Real Estate
Investor's Checklist

Other McGraw-Hill Books by Robert Irwin

Tips and Traps When Buying a Home

Tips and Traps When Selling a Home

Tips and Traps When Buying a Condo, Co-Op, or Townhouse

Tips and Traps for Making Money in Real Estate

Tips and Traps When Renovating Your Home

Tips and Traps for New Home Owners

Tips and Traps When Building Your Home

Tips and Traps When Mortgage Hunting

How to Find Hidden Real Estate Bargains

How to Buy a Home When You Can't Afford It

How to Get Started in Real Estate Investing

How to Invest in Real Estate with Little or No Money Down

Home Buyer's Checklist

Home Seller's Checklist

Home Renovation Checklist

Home Closing Checklist

Buy, Rent, and Sell

Real Estate Investor's Checklist

Everything You Need to Know to Find and Finance the Most Profitable Investment Properties

Robert Irwin

McGraw-Hill

New York   Chicago   San Francisco   Lisbon   London   Madrid   Mexico City
Milan   New Delhi   San Juan   Seoul   Singapore   Sydney   Toronto

1 2 3 4 5 6 7 8 9 0   FGR/FGR   0 9 8 7 6 5

ISBN 0-07-145646-5

This publication is designed to provide accurate and authoritative information in regard to the subject matter covered. It is sold with the understanding that neither the author nor the publisher is engaged in rendering legal, accounting, futures/securities trading, real estate, or other professional service. If legal advice or other expert assistance is required, the services of a competent professional person should be sought.

> —*From a Declaration of Principles jointly adopted by a Committee*
> *of the American Bar Association and a Committee of Publishers*

McGraw-Hill books are available at special quantity discounts to use as premiums and sales promotions, or for use in corporate training programs. For more information, please write to the Director of Special Sales, McGraw-Hill Professional, Two Penn Plaza, New York, NY 10121-2298. Or contact your local bookstore.

 This book is printed on recycled, acid-free paper containing a minimum of 50% recycled, de-inked fiber.

Library of Congress Cataloging-in-Publication Data

Irwin, Robert.
    Real estate investors checklist : everything you need to know to find and finance the most profitable investment properties / by Robert Irwin.
       p.   cm.
    Includes index.
    ISBN 0-07-145646-5 (alk. paper)
    1. Real estate investment. I. Title.
HD1382.5.I74 2006
332.63'24—dc22

                            2005030870

Contents

10. Do You Have a Good Agent?   94

Questions to Ask Yourself

Questions to Ask Your Agent

11. Is It a True Fixer-Upper?   105

Questions to Ask Yourself

Preface

WHY AN INVESTOR'S CHECKLIST BOOK?

This book (in this series) is unique. It's aimed squarely at buyers whose primary motivation in purchasing real estate is not habitat, but profit.

There are over 65 million homeowners in this country, and every one of them probably considers himself/herself a real estate investor. After all, during the last decade, if you bought a house, lived in it for a while, and then sold it, you probably made money—sometimes a lot of money. But to be a real estate investor involves more.

It means finding properties that will turn a profit either immediately or over the long haul through serial investing. It means knowing how to get the best financing. It includes understanding market cycles and knowing the optimum times to buy . . . and sell. It includes expertise in evaluating property so that you don't overpay or get stuck with a lemon. And so much more.

In short, a successful real estate investor needs more than dumb luck. He or she needs techniques that work. In the past, these were only honed from sometimes painful experience.

That's where this checklist book comes in. It has evolved from my own experiences in real estate as well as those of many other successful investors. You don't need to reinvent the wheel by making everyone else's mistakes on your way to successful real estate investing. This book gives you a list of what you need to know and then shows you how to get started doing it. It's one-stop shopping.

Try a few pages. You'll find you quickly fall into the flow of the format. You'll be picking up knowledge even as you casually read entertaining observations and commentary.

If you've always wanted to get started investing in real estate, but didn't know where to begin, even if you're already an investor with properties, you'll find that this checklist book comprehensively shows you how to do it. Just check off the paragraphs on your way to true expertise.

Robert Irwin
www.robertirwin.com

Real Estate Investor's Checklist

1
How Will You Make Your Profit?

QUESTIONS TO ASK YOURSELF

Can the property be put to a higher, better, and more profitable use? ☐

Changing the use of property is one of the oldest and smartest ways of making money in real estate. John Jacob Astor was one of the first to try it in this country in the early 1800s when he converted cow pastures in Manhattan to residential and commercial buildings, making a fortune along the way. Recently a friend I know bought an old nonproducing orange grove of 10 acres at $50,000 an acre, spending a total of half a million dollars. Then he cleared the dying trees and subdivided into lots for homes—five lots to an acre. He sold each homesite for approximately $50,000. Since he now had 50 sites, that came to $2,500,000. He made a profit of $2,000,000 before expenses (which were not insubstantial). All of this came about because he changed the usage of the property from agricultural to residential. Other changes can include small splits of a lot or home into two units instead of one (described below), or creating a big commercial usage when there was previously a multifamily residential usage. Of course, changing usage often requires approval from the local planning department, which can be anything from easy to impossible to get. However, if you do get approval for a usage change (or the property was previously zoned for a higher use), there is usually a big profit to be made. Remember, your goal as a real estate investor is to make money, and one of the fastest ways to make it is to buy a property and upgrade its use. This is an important concept that too few investors remember or fully understand. To this day, opportunities for usage change remain in most communities. For more insights into this, check out Chapter 17.

Can the property be split?

This is a case of buying one and making it into two (or more). If done right, splitting can result in substantial profit for the investor. A typical split starts with buying a large lot. Once you have ownership, you split the lot into two. Now you have two lots, which, depending on the circumstances, may each be worth nearly as much as the original lot. You sell one and have the other virtually free. Or you sell both to make your profit. (Of course, each of the lots must conform to minimum zoning size.) Variations on this theme include buying a large lot with a house on it, then selling off a portion of the lot and keeping the house as a rental. In San Francisco, where many areas are zoned for duplexes or multifamily dwellings, a split can occur when a single large home is split down the center to make a duplex (or two units). Sometimes a large home of several floors is converted to a condominium with each floor being a separate unit. Each time you split the property, you multiply your profit. A savvy investor will always be looking at properties with an eye toward being able to create a split. No, this doesn't always happen in suburbia. But it is common both in rural and in urban areas. Just be careful that you comply with all building and zoning regulations. (See also Chapter 19.)

Can the property be flipped?

Flipping is the fastest way to make money in real estate. It means selling the property for a profit as soon as you buy it, or, in some cases, even before title passes to you. I encourage you to flip a property whenever possible. It generates ready cash that can then be used for other real estate investments. However, it's important to know the limitations of flipping. (See Chapter 14.) One of the important steps in assessing an investment property is to determine its potential for flipping. Generally speaking, this is easy to do. If you can buy the property for well below market, you are in a good position to flip it. On the other hand, if you're buying close to market, unless you're in an area of very rapid price appreciation, flipping is usually not practical. Most flipping is done by two methods. One is buying an option, which is an agreement that gives you the right, but not the requirement, to purchase some time in the future. You then sell the option to a rebuyer and pocket the difference between your option price and your selling price. The other method is by assigning a purchase agreement to a rebuyer before escrow closes. In either case, you do not take ownership of the property, do not have to worry about financing it yourself, and can often make a hefty profit. Both techniques, however, can be tricky and you should use the services of a professional such as an attorney to be sure you handle them correctly.

Can the property be held?

The most common way of making money in real estate is to buy and then hold for the long term. If you look at the value of real estate over the last 60 years, you will quickly see that overall it has always gone up. (Check out the Commerce Department statistics at www.commerce.gov.) Of course, prices have declined during certain periods and in certain areas. But the trend in almost all areas is up. Thus, what many investors do is to become serial purchasers. They buy one property, rent it out, and then hold. After a time they buy another, and then another. Over years their equity increases as the tenants pay down the mortgages and the prices go up. Many millionaires in this country got started in just this fashion. (See also Chapter 14.)

Can the home be "scraped"?

Sometimes the value of a rental property is not in the building, but entirely in the land. This is often the case where prices have risen rapidly and there's an older stock of smaller homes. A good example is the San Fernando Valley near Los Angeles. Many homes were built there after the Second World War through the fifties and sixties. They tended to be smaller homes, sometimes with three bedrooms and only one bath, often under 1,500 square feet. However, because land was cheap in those days, these homes were often built on quarter acre or larger lots. Today, these houses might sell for anywhere from $400,000 to $600,000. However, if the lot is located in a desired area and a big modern home were put on it, the new house/lot could sell for many millions of dollars. Thus, another way that some investors are making money in real estate, particularly those with links to the building industry, is to buy and "scrape." Scraping means tearing down the existing home and hauling the debris away as garbage. Then, a modern new home is constructed. This is a challenging endeavor as a morass of financing, permits, and building challenges must be overcome. However, many entrepreneurs have repeatedly used this route to acquire a substantial real estate fortune. Note: Sometimes it is better to scrape only a portion of the existing home and add onto it. This is particularly the case when there are added costs involved with totally new construction, such as connecting to utilities, paying school district fees, and so on.

Can rents be raised?

The most common way of determining value in multi-family residential buildings, and in most commercial and industrial buildings as well, is by multiplying the rent. Typically, a *GIM* (or *gross income multiplier)* is used. For example, if the GIM happens to be 12 and the gross annual income from rents for a project is $150,000, then the approximate purchase price should be $1,800,000. (Just multiply $150,000 times 12.) What should be obvious is that if you can raise the rent and the multiplier stays constant, you can increase the value of the property. For example, if you buy the building for $1.8 million and then double the rents to $300,000 annually, when you apply the GIM again, you come up with a figure of $3.6 million. Thus, for savvy investors an important evaluation of a property is to see whether or not the rents can be raised. Many a small fortune has been found by purchasing a building in which the tenants were paying rents that hadn't been raised in years and were well below market. A new investor buys the property, raises the rents to market price (which may involve replacing some tenants), and then resells for a healthy profit. Of course, if rents are initially low, it's important to determine why. Sometimes it can be because of a big detracting feature, in other cases the property may be run down and need maintenance and repair. (Of course, yet another way to profit is to buy an older "fixer-upper," do the work, raise the rents, and resell at a profit.) (Also, check out Chapter 8.)

Are there any lease advantages (or restrictions)?

Many properties are rented on a month-to-month basis. That simply means that either the landlord or the tenant may terminate the rental usually with a month's notice. However, other times real estate is rented on a lease basis. A lease has a defined time period for which the property is rented, typically a year or more. When you buy a property that has leases on it, the leases run with the land. That means that they don't end simply because there's a change of title. Therefore, it's important to determine if the leases will enhance or restrict your ability to raise rents, to remodel units, or to otherwise change the financial and physical structure of the building. For example, you may find a building in which the rents are very low. You want to buy it, raise rents, and sell for a profit. However, the tenants are all on long-term leases. These leases do not call for rent increases. Thus, if you buy the building you'll be stuck with those low-paying tenants until the leases expire. For this reason, the price may remain low. However, a creative investor may buy low and then offer the existing tenants a bonus to move out, after which he or she rerents to higher-paying tenants. Checking out the leases is vitally important when buying rental real estate. Sometimes it can be the road to riches. (Also, check out Chapter 16.)

Can the security deposits be an advantage?

Getting a security deposit is common with rental real estate. For example, you own a home that you're renting out. You insist that the tenant pay one or more months' rent up front as security against moving out without paying rent that's due. By its very nature, a deposit is refundable. In most cases the deposit must be returned when the tenant moves out leaving the property in good shape. When you purchase a building, you—as the new owner—are responsible for all of the security deposits that all of the tenants have paid to the seller. In a multifamily dwelling of 25 units where each tenant has paid $1,500 in a security deposit, that's upwards of $37,500—a not insubstantial amount of money. Therefore, as the buyer you should collect those deposits from the seller. (Usually they are paid to you as a credit in escrow.) Yes, you'll eventually need to pay the deposits back. But in the meantime, they are often cash for you that can help with the purchase. Indeed, some savvy entrepreneurs have leveraged the security deposits on buildings to cover their down payments when making purchases! (See also Chapter 12.)

Can I get a better price because of poor condition?

Sometimes, properties, whether single-family detached homes, multiple-unit dwellings, or commercial property, can be bought for a much lower than market price because of their deteriorated condition. This is usually the case when an owner/seller has put off necessary maintenance and repair work for many years. These are commonly referred to as "fixer-uppers" or "handyman specials." Some real estate investors specialize in this facet of the market. They buy rundown properties, fix them up, and then either resell quickly for a profit or hold for years collecting ever higher rents. In your analysis of a property, it's important to determine if it's a good purchase because of its poor condition. Does that condition allow you to buy low? Be aware, however, that buying rundown properties has its challenges. These include the time, effort, and cost of bringing the property up to standard. One of the biggest mistakes an investor can make is to purchase a rundown property for under market cost only to realize later that by the time the costs of fixing up are added on, the total cost is above market. Buy only if you can get it cheap enough.

Can I get a better price because of poor location?

Sometimes an investor can purchase a property for a very low price because it's in a bad location. Then the investor can help improve the neighborhood or somehow change the property's relation to it, and in this way increase the property's value. In this situation, it's important to keep in mind the risk. If the price is low mainly because of a poor location and you can't effect a change, you might have to accept a low price when you sell. Thus, when location is an issue, the most important thing is to determine if you as the new owner can do anything to mitigate the problem. For example, say you want to purchase a home as a rental and the price is low, but it's right behind a shopping mall with its attendant traffic and noise. However, if you buy the property and are able to erect a fence that shields it from the mall, you might be able to reduce significantly the detracting influence and thus be able to sell without being at a disadvantage. Similarly, some investors have been able to effectively change the detracting feature itself. For example, they have bought homes in neighborhoods where the prices were driven down because the neighboring homes were poorly kept up. They then formed a homeowner's association, which went around and helped clean up the bad properties. Once the neighborhood was ship-shape, they were able to resell for a healthy profit. It's important for every investor to determine if there's a problem with the location of the subject property. If there is, then it's equally important to determine if anything can be done about that problem and what risks there are of not being able to effect a remedy. Buying low because of location and later being able to sell high because you have in some way remedied the problem can be a profitable approach to dealing in real estate.

Can I buy with little or no cash?

Sometimes institutional lenders will offer financing deals in which no down payment is needed. These deals can also include limited or no closing costs. Taking advantage can quickly get you into the real estate game. If considering these deals, first check with a good mortgage broker. Other times, sellers are desperate to sell and will carry back financing (paper). You may be able to get a reduced interest rate and other concessions from a truly desperate seller along with little or no money down. In other circumstances you can use a "land contract of sale" or an option to purchase. Just be sure you use a lawyer and have the contract recorded to protect yourself. Or you may even end up using a promissory note in lieu of a down payment. The list of ways to purchase with little or no cash is limited only by your imagination. But, in all cases, be sure that you end up with a property that can show you a profit. Simply being able to buy a property isn't enough. You have to buy a property that either can be quickly resold (flipped) or can make you money over the long haul through a positive cash flow. (See also Chapter 2.)

2

What Do You Need to Get Started?

QUESTIONS TO ASK YOURSELF

How much cash do I need?

It really depends on what you intend to buy. The bigger the property, generally speaking, the more cash required for the down payment and the closing costs. If you're buying a $10 million commercial building, you might need $1 million or more in cash. (Of course, there are always amazing tales of the financing of huge deals with virtually no cash—but don't count on it happening every time.) On the other hand, if you're buying a single-family house or condo, you might need very little down, plus closing costs. If you're buying a home you plan to live in and then, after a period of time such as a year or two, rent out as an investment, you may need nothing down. Nothing down financing (sometimes including closing costs) is readily available for buyers who intend to be owner/occupants. (This is probably the easiest way for the average person to get started investing in real estate.) Nonetheless, it's better to have some money rather than no money when you're a beginning investor. Even a few thousand dollars will be enough to smooth out the rough spots in a transaction.

Where can I get the money?

The easiest method is simply to write a check from your own account, which is bulging with cash. Don't have such an account? Don't feel bad—neither do most of us. If you need money to get started investing in real estate, there are a variety of sources. First off, remember that most real estate purchased by investors is heavily leveraged. That means that usually an institutional lender (or sometimes a seller) is already financing most of the purchase. For investors, loans up to 90 percent of *LTV* (*loan to value*) are often available. For owner occupants, as noted above, the LTV goes to 100 percent and sometimes 103 to 125 percent! (See a good mortgage broker for details or read *Tips & Traps When Mortgage Hunting*, McGraw-Hill, 2005.) If you do need money for a down payment and closing costs, your sources can include gifts from relatives and/or friends, selling some of your assets, and borrowing on other property or even on credit cards. (See Chapter 19 for more details.)

What's my ability to get financing?

Knowing that 90 to 100 percent LTV real estate loans are available is not the same as knowing that you can get one. The important thing is to line up your financing *before* you get involved in a deal. You don't want to be scrambling around trying to find a lender and, in so doing, jeopardize an otherwise good purchase. If you're an experienced investor, you'll certainly have lenders with whom you've worked in the past who can help you out on the current deal. If you're a new investor, however, even before looking at property, find a good mortgage broker with whom to work. The mortgage broker can get you preapproved by a lender. That will tell you how much you can afford to borrow. It will also clue you in as to what types of mortgages are available to investors at the time you're hunting and what interest rate you'll need to pay. (Sometimes investors have to pay a higher interest rate than owner occupants.) If you intend to start out by living in the property for a time before converting it to a rental, the mortgage broker can secure the very best financing in the world for you. You can find mortgage brokers in the phone book and online. I suggest you use online services to get generic information on mortgages and interest rates. But deal with a mortgage broker in person your first time out. It will make it much easier for you, and for the broker, to tailor financing to just your needs.

Will I have the time to devote to real estate investing?

I and many others have found that the best way to invest in real estate is to do it on the side and in your spare time. The reason is that you probably won't have much positive cash flow in the early years. That means you'll need to keep your regular job. This leaves your spare time for investing. Married investors sometimes keep one spouse working full-time while the other dabbles in property. In addition to maintaining a steady of flow of income, this also often provides job benefits such as health insurance. As a real estate investor, you're on your own in terms of all the niceties that being an employee offers. The beauty, of course, is that real estate doesn't require full-time work. In fact, if you plan on doing nothing more than spending 5 or 10 hours a week on your real estate investments, you should thrive in the field. On the other hand, the time you spend will probably not be at your convenience. When a good deal suddenly appears, you have to be ready to take advantage of it. That means being ready to make an offer any time—morning, afternoon, or evening. And once you own property and become a landlord, you're going to be at the beck and call of your tenants.

Do I have a team?

Team investing is now in vogue, and for good reason. It's most unlikely that any one individual will have all the skills and resources necessary to build a real estate empire. (The one exception is serial investing as described above.) If you're going to quickly acquire many properties, flip homes, invest in fixer-uppers, delve into commercial real estate and land, you'd better be expert in all of those areas. You're not? Then build a team that is. A good team usually includes an agent, an attorney (or someone with experience and knowledge of real estate law), a builder (or even a carpenter, but a person who knows construction), a specialist in leases (often a commercial agent), and one or more entrepreneurs (who can be you if you don't fit the other categories). This is a team that can find good investment properties and accurately analyze them in terms of their profit potential and how to turn them over. Having a team also means that you'll probably have access to far more in financial resources than you would alone. Building a team requires a "spark plug," one person who solicits and pulls together all the other team members. If no one has asked you to join a team, then it's probably up to you to form one. It's not hard to do, since most people welcome the opportunity. There is, however, one important caution. Don't form a team of just your friends. Pick your associates because of what they can bring to the team, not because you happen to know them well. And, of course, always look for honesty as the number one requirement. Many teams work on a handshake, but the best policy is to have an attorney draw up a partnership agreement that specifies who contributes what, and how the profits are divided.

Do I have the right mindset?

There's business. And then there's your personal life. It's a challenge to keep the two separate when you march into real estate investing. For one thing, you'll have to have the discipline to spend weekends and evenings looking at property and then handling maintenance and repairs as needed. For another, you'll need to separate your own likes and distastes from what you need to do to succeed. This is important because most of us look at property only on the basis of how nice it would be to live in it. Perhaps we see a wonderful marble entryway with glass front doors. But, marble scratches easily and glass breaks. How practical are those features in a rental? (Of course, a lot depends on the overall quality of the home and the size of the security deposit.) Finally, as a real estate investor, you'll be buying property from people in divorce and from probate sales. You'll be dealing with tenants who cry because they can't come up with the rent, who have lost a job and have no money. Your heart may go out to the people you deal with. But, if you make their problem yours by giving them a better deal or letting the rent slip, you'll pay for it the hard way—with money out of your pocket. You don't have to be a hard case to invest in real estate. But you have to be able to separate personal wishes and desires from business. It's a business and requires a mindset that understands this. You need to see property with an investor's eye.

Do I have the right personality type?

Some personality traits are a plus in real estate. For example, are you a *detail* person? You'll need to keep track of market values, of rents received and expenses paid out, of interest rates and loan payment dates, of items needing repair and those that can last a bit longer. There are hundreds of details in real estate investing (indeed in most other endeavors) and you need to be able to keep track of all of them to succeed. Also, you'll need to have people skills. While it's true that some real estate investors are reclusive (Howard Hughes being the best example that comes to mind), most are gregarious and are interested in people. The skills you have in dealing with others will come into play when you negotiate with buyers, sellers, tenants, and agents. I have a friend who owns nearly 100 properties and is wonderful in dealing with tenants. He never raises his voice and never threatens. He simply points out the facts: the rent must come first; if it isn't paid, it will affect the tenant's credit; and it could ultimately result in the tenant being evicted. He shows the tenant why it's to his or her advantage to pay the rent. The ability to pay attention to detail and possessing people skills as well are a definite plus.

3

Did You Evaluate the Market before Entering?

QUESTIONS TO ASK YOURSELF

Is now a good time to invest in real estate?

☐

Some people feel that it's always a good time to buy real estate. But often these are people (such as agents) who depend on a steady stream of sales for their income. Investors, however, need to be more discriminating. Historically, real estate goes through up and down cycles. A great time to buy is when the market has just gotten off a low and prices are beginning to rise. You can buy almost anything and ride the boom to profits. On the other hand, buying right after the market has peaked is not necessarily a good idea. No matter how good a bargain you may get, you could find that you'll have trouble reselling quickly at a profit because of stagnant or even falling prices. Timing your investment to coincide with real estate market conditions can mean the difference between success and failure. Of course, if you plan to buy and hold for the long term, then over time the ups and downs of the market will tend to even out, and you should end up with a very valuable piece of property. But, if that's your goal, be sure that you know how to buy right so that you don't have negative cash flow.

Is it a good time to flip properties?

☐

The fastest way to make money in residential real estate is to flip properties. This means that you sell them soon after (within weeks or months) purchasing. Or you sell them in escrow even before you take title. (See Chapter 14 for flipping techniques.) However, not all markets support flipping. The best time is when the market is superheated and prices are rising rapidly. The worst time is when there's a real estate recession and prices are declining. Simply telling yourself you want to get into flipping isn't enough. To be successful you must also do a thorough analysis of the market.

Are sellers motivated to take lowball offers?

One way to create bargains in real estate is to make low offers on properties. It's the old story of buying low and then selling high. Many successful investors will make a series of lowball offers on different properties, perhaps 10 or more, in the hope of getting just one seller to accept. However, it's important to understand that sellers are not usually willing to accept lowball offers when there's a strong market. They know that if they don't sell low to you, chances are that another buyer will quickly come along with a better price. Your best chance of getting sellers to accept lowball offers on good properties is in a stagnant market (neither declining nor increasing in price) where there's a large inventory and it takes a long time to sell a home. Look for sellers who've had their properties on the market for several months and are getting eager to move. Beware of making lowball offers in a declining market. When prices are falling, your lowball offer of today could turn out to be a high price tomorrow as the market moves further down.

Am I competing with many other investors?

As an investor, you never operate in a vacuum. There are always others out there who are trying to get the same good deal you're going after. Usually, however, it's the early bird that gets the worm. Work diligently on finding properties and you'll get your share of good ones. Keep in mind, however, that sometimes the number of investors increases dramatically as speculators get into the market. This typically happens at the end of a real estate cycle as prices blow out to the high end. Suddenly everyone seems to understand the value of having a rental home or two. And even those who don't normally invest in real estate begin thinking about flipping. Often, it's best to wait on the sidelines when the competition heats up, or else you'll find yourself in bidding wars that may result in your paying too much for a property.

Can I afford to get into the local market?

It's important to know what you can afford. For example, there are some stores in which you may be able to afford any product on the shelf, such as the "99 cent stores." On the other hand, there may be other stores, such as Tiffany's, where you can afford only one or two items, or perhaps none at all. Real estate markets are similar. In some you'll be able to pick and choose from a host of homes. In others, you'll only be able to afford a starter home, if that. As an investor, it's usually best to get started in a market where you have a choice of homes that you can afford. That way you're not limited to buying only the cheapest house for sale. If the market in which you're living is unaffordable for you, you might want to consider moving to a less expensive one. (The coasts tend to average many times higher in price for homes than the middle of the country.) Because there is so much money to be made in real estate over the long run, it's not unusual for savvy investors to pick up and move to an area where they can more easily afford to start investing.

Are rents high enough to buy and hold?

While flipping is the fastest way to make money in real estate, buying and holding is the surest. The formula is quite simple, and literally millions of investors have profited from it. You just buy a property and hold (rent it out) for years. Over time, the tenants pay off the mortgage and inflation increases its value. Over several decades, your investment can make you wealthy, particularly if you own several such properties. The trick, however, is to find properties whose rental income will cover your basic expenses—at the least, PITI (principal, interest, taxes, and insurance). Although you may still have to take money out of pocket to cover vacancies, clean up, rent up, maintenance, and repairs, tax breaks could help to cover some or all of these costs. (See Chapter 18 on taxation.) The problem is that properties will very often rent for much less than PITI, resulting in a strong "negative cash flow," which means you'll need to take money out of your pocket each month to keep the properties solvent. No investor wants to see this, and very few can sustain it for years. Therefore, it's critical that, unless you're convinced you can flip the property, you make very sure that the rents in the area are high enough to cover your basic costs.

QUESTIONS TO RESEARCH

Where are we in the real estate cycle?

As with most investment fields, real estate tends to have a cyclical market. Some years it's up, and other years it's down. In watching the market for over four decades and checking the statistics on price changes at the Commerce Department (www.commerce.org), it's become clear to me that the real estate market tends to move in 7-year/14-year cycles. Historically, it has gone up, or down, for about 7 years before switching directions. Typically, a complete cycle (apex to base to apex) takes about 14 years. While these are not exact figures, and they might not be duplicated in future markets, they are a good starting point to help identify where the current market is. If real estate has been "hot" for 5 or 6 years, chances are it's getting ready to peak and may soon be turning down. If it's been cold for 5 or 6 years, it may be getting ready to reverse direction and turn up. It's critical to peg the location of the market in the current cycle since you don't want to buy just as it turns down, or sell just as it turns up.

How are the state and local economies doing with jobs?

Home prices follow jobs. Economic statistics are widely reported in both national and local newspapers. Read papers such as the *Wall Street Journal* or the *New York Times* regularly, and you should get a handle on where the national economy is. Read local newspapers for statistics in your area and neighborhood. If the national and local economies are tanking, chances are there will be a loss of jobs. And that will eventually result in a deterioration of the overall real estate market. On the other hand, if the national and, particularly, the local economies are booming, expect real estate prices to go up as new jobs bring in new workers and home buyers. Be wary of investing in a weakening economy.

What is the local supply/demand for housing?

All real estate is local. If there are more houses than buyers, prices will tend to fall. If there are more buyers than houses, prices will tend to rise. Nationally, the supply of housing decreased significantly between 1995 and 2005 because of a slow down in construction. However, in a few local markets, such as those experiencing a loss of jobs, this trend was reversed. The Commerce Department (www.commerce.gov) and the National Association of Home Builders (www.nahb.org) put out statistics for home supply/demand. Other organizations may do it for your area. (Check an Internet search engine such as Google for information on your location by looking up key terms such as *housing supply* and *residential supply/demand*.) In the Los Angeles market, for example, which covers a huge amount of territory, there is relatively little buildable land available. Hence there is a shortage of housing that has resulted in past price increases. In other areas, such as Las Vegas, there are enormous tracts of buildable land, meaning that the potential supply is almost endless. While the short supply in Los Angeles bodes well for sustained price increases, the abundant supply in Las Vegas suggests that over time there will be increased market volatility. As of this writing the Las Vegas market is the hottest in the country. But it is supported by many new arrivals in the area and by many speculators. This is leading to building in huge new areas that, in time, could reverse the situation.

Are there many REOs in the market?

REO stands for "real estate owned," and it refers to homes that lenders, such as banks, have taken back through foreclosure. The presence of a host of REOs suggests that owner/borrowers have neither had the means nor the will to keep their properties when times got tough. The more REOs in the market, generally speaking, the weaker it is. On the other hand, "working the REOs" can be a good opportunity for investors. (Read Chapter 9.) It is sometimes possible to buy an REO for under market (usually if it's in bad shape), fix it up, and then quickly resell—a kind of flipping. This will work in all but the worst market conditions. Finding good REOs, however, often means having a contact in a bank. You should check with your local bank to see if it has any REOs in the area. (Most banks farm their REOs out to local agents.)

Are many sellers "upside down"?

Being "upside down" simply means that you owe more on your home than it's worth. Getting into this condition can come about in a variety of different ways. For example, a buyer who purchases using a "125 percent" mortgage (the loan is for more than the home's value) is immediately upside down. Buyers who purchase using adjustable-rate mortgages (ARMs), particularly those who purchase with nothing down and interest-only loans (which typically convert to ARMs within a few years), can quickly become upside down if interest rates go up. A declining real estate market, of course, is the most likely way owners get to be upside down. When there are many homeowners who are upside down, it's a bad sign for the market and indicates prices are likely to be falling. While this is generally a poor time to invest, it can also be an opportunity for investors if they can buy using a "short payoff" (where the lender accepts far less than the full mortgage amount just to be rid of the property). Ask a good mortgage broker about the number of owners who are upside down in your area.

Are there many FSBOs in the market?

Properties for sale by owner (FSBOs) are indicators of two kinds of markets. One is a very hot market where sellers are concluding that properties sell so fast they don't need an agent. Hence, they list with themselves. The other is a very slow market where sellers have had little success in selling through an agent and now, in desperation, are trying to sell by themselves. When there are relatively few FSBOs, it suggests that the market is relatively calm, appreciating slowly. You can simply drive down neighborhoods you are considering and count up the number of FSBOs. That should give you a good indication of where the market in your area is.

QUESTIONS TO ASK AN AGENT

How big an inventory of unsold homes is there?

The housing inventory refers to all the homes that are for sale at any given time within a local area. This inventory will swell or reduce at different times. It is an excellent indicator of both how strong the market is and the direction in which it's going. The inventory is expressed in a variety of ways, one of which is the total number of homes for sale. Another more useful way of expressing inventory is in how many months or days it will take to sell out the entire inventory of homes at the current rate of sales. (Of course, new homes are constantly coming onto the market so the inventory is never completely exhausted.) In a very hot market, the time to sell out typically is less than 60 days, sometimes less than 30 days! In a cold market, it's typically six months and sometimes far longer. When inventory is high, it suggests that there are too many houses on the market and sellers can't sell—a good time to find bargains. When inventory is low, it suggests there are too many buyers competing in the market and it will be tough finding a house at a reasonable price—and there may be multiple offers on any bargains. Also, the trend in inventory is important. Are there month-to-month increases or decreases in inventory? Increases suggest a sagging market; decreases suggest a tightening market where price appreciation is likely. Be sure to check the month-to-month changes going back at least a year or two to get an understanding of where your market really is. You can get this information from almost any real estate agent. Virtually all real estate boards track market inventory, and an agent can usually give you all the statistics you need just by tapping a few keys on the office computer. This is normally a free service performed in the hope of eventually getting you to list or buy through the agent.

What's the time needed to sell the average home?

This is an often used but rarely understood statistic. It is derived by comparing the inventory to the rate of home sales. For example, say there are typically around 400 homes sold each month. And the inventory currently consists of 1,600 homes. It will sell out within four months. That's the *maximum* time it should take to sell the average home, assuming it shows well, is priced right, and so on. However, since the average home is by definition in the middle of the pack, you could expect it to sell sooner. Some homes will take four months to sell, others will sell immediately, and the average should be in the middle. Thus, in our example, the average home could be expected to sell within two months. (Note: Not all agents and investors calculate it in this fashion, but instead use the time to sell out the entire inventory for determining how long it will take to sell the average home.) Again, you can make this calculation after getting the statistics from an agent (see above). The importance of "the time to sell" is that it's another tool in determining how strong the market is and where it's headed. Comparing month-to-month "time to sell" going back six months should clearly indicate whether the market is strengthening, weakening, or stagnating. Also, very short or very long times to sell indicate super heated or deadly cold market conditions.

Are there many repos in the market?

Few people will let their house go to repossession, whatever the circumstances, in a hot market. Why should they? It's so easy to just put it up for sale, find a buyer, and sell your way out of foreclosure. On the other hand, when the market's very slow, it can be difficult, if not downright impossible, to sell quickly and avoid foreclosure. Thus, the number of homes in foreclosure at any given time is a strong clue as to the market's condition. You can determine the homes in foreclosure by asking a savvy agent who is on top of the market. You can also go to Web sites that specialize in foreclosures, such as www.foreclosures.com or www.4close.com. And you can check national statistics at the Department of Commerce (www.commerce.gov).

Keep in mind, however, that all real estate is local, and the fact that the number of foreclosures is high or low nationally may not reflect your particular area. Also keep in mind that when there are lots of foreclosures on the market, it's an excellent time to drive a hard bargain with sellers. Real estate investors who take the risks and buy up property that's in foreclosure but not yet taken back by lenders (as opposed to buying REOs as discussed above) often do a highly lucrative business, even though they are sometimes disparagingly referred to a "bottom feeders." Be careful here, as there are many pitfalls.

Are there multiple offers on homes?

This is such an amazing phenomenon that when it happens, it's often the subject of news stories. Two or more buyers bid at the same time for the same house. Often these multiple offers result in prices being bid up far above what the seller was asking—a definite plus for the seller, but unless the buyer is very savvy about market prices, usually a minus for the purchaser. Multiple offers only occur in two ways. The most common is in a very hot market with limited inventory. The competition for housing is fierce and buyers bid against one another for good properties. The other situation can occur in any market, and it's when two buyers independently decide to buy a property at the same time. Multiple offers are almost always a symptom of a very hot market, one in which it will be difficult to get sellers to cut their prices. You aren't likely to find many bargains here. Although, as suggested, savvy buyers may realize a home is actually underpriced, engage in a bidding war, and still get the home for below market. (Be wary of sellers who purposely underprice their homes in order to start a bidding war with the hope that eventually they will get a higher than market price.) Many investors simply prefer to sit it out on the sidelines where multiple offers are common. Agents can tell you if multiple offers are the rule in your market. But be sure to check with a few agents to get the whole picture. One agent may see only a portion of the market or, in rare cases, an unscrupulous agent might seek to get you to make a higher offer by intimating multiple offers are common when they aren't.

Are sellers cutting their prices?

The opposite of a market in which there are multiple offers is one in which there are few to no offers. This indicates a weak market, one where prices are stagnating or even falling. It's the place where a savvy investor can come in with lowball offers and hope to get them accepted. It's a bargain hunter's paradise. (Beware, however, of getting your low-ball price only to find the market dropping below it!) Also, sometimes sellers will cut their prices even in a hot market simply because they started out too high. Ask agents whether price cuts are a common occurrence or a rarity.

In which direction are interest rates going?

Real estate tends to be interest-rate sensitive. When rates rise, so do mortgage payments, which means that fewer people can qualify for a big mortgage to buy an expensive home. As a result, the demand for these properties slips . . . and so, too, does the market. The opposite occurs when interest rates fall. More people can afford to buy more expensive properties, and prices tend to rise. Keep in mind, however, that the market can often absorb a rise or fall of between 1 and 2 percent in interest rates before a major change in the real estate market occurs. The best rate to follow is the one for the 30-year fixed-rate mortgage (without points). This rate is widely reported in all major newspapers, as well as at online sources such as www.eloan.com and www.hsh.com.

4

Did You Check the Neighborhood before Making an Offer?

QUESTIONS TO ASK YOURSELF

Is it a good location?

☐

Everyone knows that the cubed watchword of real estate is *location*. But what makes a property a good investment location? The rules for residential real estate are somewhat different from those of commercial, industrial, land, or other types of real property. They involve such things as schools, crime, tenant base, and more. Before buying an investment home, even if you've already found one you like, be sure to check out its location carefully. Nothing will make you regret your purchase more than to have a bad location. And nothing will help you to obtain greater profits than a good location.

Is it close to home?

☐

This is a seemingly strange question to ask. Is the subject property located close to your residence? But it's extremely important as any savvy investor will tell you. It all comes down to personal service. With residential investment real estate, unless you're the owner of a large apartment complex who can afford a management company, chances are you're the one who's going to be doing the renting, the maintenance and repairs, and the fielding of tenant questions and complaints, all of which means that you'll probably want and need to go down to the property frequently. That's an easy task if it's only half an hour or so away from

your home. It becomes an increasingly more difficult task
the further away the property is. Owning rental real estate
that is hours away from your home or, God forbid, a plane
ride away, is like the kiss of death. You'll be hounded by
your inability to deal adequately with the property. And, if
you in desperation resort to a distant property management firm, you'll find that the fees strain your pocketbook.
Don't underestimate this problem or think it's being exaggerated. I made this mistake myself early on in my real
estate career and sorely regretted it. Never buy a rental
property that's more than an hour away from your home.
(Half an hour away is even better!) If there's nothing else
you take away from this book, heed this! Buy close to
home. (See Chapter 9 on possible solutions when properties close to home are too expensive.)

Am I comfortable going there to collect rent?

Again, it's important to understand the personal nature
of owning residential real estate. Until you become a
tycoon who can afford an expensive management company, chances are you'll be the one to collect the rent. And
the question becomes, "Will you be comfortable going
there to collect it?" Sometimes bargain real estate is
located in dangerous neighborhoods. You might find that
you can get the house at a "steal." But what good is that if
you're afraid someone will mug you or steal your rent
every time you go to collect it? You may gather all the
crime statistics on the neighborhood you like (see the next
question), but it all comes down to whether or not you're
willing to make the trek to collect the rent. And don't
assume that you can have the tenants mail it to you. There
will come times when showing up at the door may be the
only way to get it. And don't forget the time you'll need
to spend repairing and doing maintenance, showing the
property to tenants, and so on. Always buy in a neighborhood that you won't mind visiting day or night. You
might end up paying more, but you'll also end up sleep-
ing more comfortably when you think about it.

What is the "graffiti index"?

One way to help determine the quality of a location is to
check to see how much graffiti there is on neighborhood

walls and fences. Some graffiti is to be expected in almost any neighborhood. But if the fences and walls of nearby homes and parks are covered with it, it suggests a number of ominous things. First, if the graffiti stays there for long without being cleaned up or painted over, it indicates a low level of neighborhood pride. In strong neighborhoods, homeowners are out there right away to remove the graffiti. And studies have shown that in areas where it is rapidly removed, it tends to stay away. Taggers who paint it really don't like to see their handiwork cleaned up quickly and will often go elsewhere. Lots of graffiti may also suggest a criminal element is at work in the neighborhood. Some neighborhood gangs do good work for their community. But others are composed of gangster types who inform others of their illicit activities through graffiti. In order to successfully rent out your home, you might have to come to some sort of accommodation with them. Is that something you're prepared to deal with? If not, then check out the "graffiti index" and stay away from locations where it's high.

What is the mix of tenants to owners?

It's important to understand that those who own their houses usually have "pride of ownership." Those who rent obviously do not. This means that where owners might put in new front yards or repaint their homes, tenants are most likely simply to let it go and ask the investor/owner to do it. There's nothing wrong with this. You can't really expect tenants to take care of a property they don't own. After all, it's the owner, not the tenant, who reaps the rewards when the home is sold (not to mention tax advantages). Hence, it's the owner who normally has the burden of maintenance, repairs, and improvements. Unfortunately, many investors are unwilling or do not have the funds to properly maintain and improve their investment properties. The results can be weed-strewn front yards, dilapidated buildings, chipped and weathered paint, and so on. In many neighborhoods, you can tell the investment properties from the owner-occupied ones simply by walking by and seeing which look good and which look bad. Too many rundown investment properties can drag a neighborhood down. It can adversely affect prices, make it more difficult to find tenants, and result in long delays when selling. Therefore, before buying in any neighborhood, you should walk it. Walk not only the block on which the subject home is located, but all the nearby streets as well. You'll know what you're looking for when you see it. It's the dilapidated run-down house that needs work. No, it's not necessarily an investor's house, but there's a good chance it is. If there are more than one or two in the immediate area, reconsider your purchase. Remember, you don't own property in a vacuum, and buyers and tenants make the selection based not only on a house, but on a neighborhood.

Are all the homes and landscaping kept up?

In the question above we noted that "pride of ownership" is usually a component of a good neighborhood. But not always. Some owners just don't care. In some neighborhoods, the owners will park cars on their front lawns, change oil in their driveways, let their pets roam freely, and, in extreme cases, even throw their garbage into the street. While this is rare, particularly in recent years when home price increases have made almost every owner appreciate his or her property more, it does happen. And it can happen in the best of neighborhoods. Again, before you make your purchase, walk the streets. Sometimes it only takes one bad owner to turn the neighborhood into an eyesore. If there are several who don't take care of their property, the street can very quickly begin to look like a slum. Don't make the mistake of thinking that the errant homeowners will change their ways after you buy. Without the influence of a strong homeowners' association, there's very little that an individual homeowner can do to clean up his or her neighbor's actions. Assume the worst—the neighborhood will stay the same as it is when you buy or may actually go downhill a bit. If the subject property is still a bargain, you may want to go ahead and make an offer. But be sure your offer is low enough to allow you room to escape quickly at a low resale price if you can't stand the nearby owners.

Would I be willing to live in it?

This is a trick question, but an important one to ask. It's tricky because it's usually a mistake to buy only investment property that you'd be willing to live in. You may have penthouse tastes, but there are very many profitable basement rentals out there. Buy just to your tastes, and you could be missing out on a whole segment of the market. The investor who only seeks out property where he or she would be willing to live is likely to be very limited in finding suitable properties. On the other hand, each investor has a style. (It may take a while, but over time you'll find your own style developing.) Some investors prefer properties in better, more expensive locations. Other investors look for properties with views. Still others seek out properties with expensive amenities such as stained wood floors, granite countertop kitchens, and so on. And yet other investors look for a plain and simple home that they can quickly and cheaply come into and repaint and recarpet after a tenant leaves. You'll find that you'll do better as a landlord/investor if you identify the type of home you're comfortable with—your style of home—and stick with it. When you're just starting out, sometimes it's simply easier to look for an investment home you'd be willing to live in (even if it's smaller, less elegant, not as well located, and so on, as your present residence).

QUESTIONS TO ASK AUTHORITIES

Is there strong local job growth?

Growth in the housing market follows growth in the employment market. The whole country may seem to be booming, but if the area you are in is losing jobs, chances are the housing market is in the dumps. Fortunately, local and state governments tend to keep accurate track of employment rates. You can check with your state and city governments' economic planning office. Be sure to look for employment *projections* in your area. The present is important, but if you're planning to buy and hold, it's the future that's going to be of greatest concern to you. Sometimes you can get real bargains in areas where the current employment is low, but where projections show it to be rising soon because of the arrival of new industries (and jobs).

What is the crime rate on the street?

No neighborhood is absolutely crime free. But some neighborhoods have less crime than others. Those are the ones that most people want to live in. It's important to remember that, as an investor in housing, you are bridging two markets—one is investment and the other is habitat. When it comes time to sell your house or condo, chances are you won't be selling it to another investor, you'll be selling it to a person who plans to occupy it. And chances are that homebuyer will be most interested in purchasing in a low-crime area. (If you're purchasing multifamily, the rules are only slightly different. Most tenants look for buildings that are located in lower-crime areas.) Therefore, it pays to check out the crime statistics for the neighborhood with care. These are normally available by calling the local police department. (Ask for the Community Affairs Officer.) Typically, the police will provide reports right down to the block in which your subject house is located. Checking these out before you leap in and purchase can save you a whole lot of trouble later on when you're trying to find good tenants and when you're eventually trying to resell. One additional word of caution: Beware of purchasing property that was previously used as a location where drugs were sold. Old habits die hard and you may find addicts coming back to the property over time. This could disrupt your current tenants and work against a profitable resale. Again, the police can provide detailed information here. Note that if your home is used for the sale of drugs, even without your knowledge, it can be seized by the federal government with little recourse for you.

What are the test scores in local schools?

Today, all schools in the country from first grade through high school conduct standardized testing of their students. The overall scores (not those of any individual student) are normally made available to the public. You should make every effort to check these out. The scores are typically given as a percentage of 100. Keep in mind that many studies have shown that the single biggest influence on property values within an area is the quality of schools. Buy in an area that has high percentile scores and you'll find there are more tenants and more buyers when it eventually comes time to resell. Buy in an area where the scores are low, and you'll find the property prices tend to appreciate more slowly; it's harder to get good tenants; and it's harder to resell. Make it a point to visit the district office of your local schools and ask to see the test score results. Use them as an important tool when determining whether or not to buy the property.

Is this a redevelopment area?

Some investors make it a point to buy cheap properties in distressed neighborhoods. They then do very little maintenance and repair and rent them out ruthlessly. The result may be a short-term profit. However, in the long run the properties usually decay to the point where they require major renovation . . . or must be abandoned, ultimately resulting in a loss. On the other hand, other investors buy similar properties in areas that are being redeveloped. Here there may be government funds available for refurbishing the dwellings. In addition, private investors may be sinking their own money into buildings. In a successful redevelopment area, you can see positive change occurring in the neighborhood almost on a daily basis. In fact, some of the biggest money made in real estate today is in redevelopment, typically in inner city areas. (Because of crowding and traffic congestion in outer city areas, older inner city neighborhoods are becoming increasingly popular, particularly to a younger generation of homeowners and tenants.) To find out about redevelopment areas in your city, check with your planning commission. Look for a "Master Plan Map" that should give the boundaries of the redevelopment area. Check with Housing and Urban Development (www.hud.gov) about federal funding in the area. Also ask at the city manager's office about local funding.

What new developments are in the planning stages?

WalMart may be coming to town. Or a new factory to churn out autos or televisions may be in the works. A new highway could be planned for the next few years that will open up an entire section of the city that's previously had limited access. Perhaps there's a big resort planned near the river or the mountains. The one thing that's constant in communities is change. People and companies are always doing something to change the landscape of the community. And by buying ahead of this "progress," you can position yourself for big profits. (Two hundred years ago John Jacob Astor bought pastureland on the outskirts of Manhattan and raked in a fortune when it was converted to business and residential use. You can do the same.) Check with your local planning department. The idea is to go down on a slow day and bend the ear of one of the clerks. Ask about big new projects in the works. An agreeable clerk can tell you all about what's going on and even provide maps, environmental reports, and more. (It's all public information.) Most developments take years to be built, so that gives you plenty of time to get ahead of the curve. You may also want to check out back issues of the local newspaper. If you go down to the newspaper office (or online where available), you can often search for articles by topic and geographical location. Going back a few years, you may be able to gain profitable information about the future.

QUESTIONS TO ASK AN AGENT

What is the mix of tenants to owners?

It seems a paradox, but the best rentals are those that are in neighborhoods where there are *fewer* rental properties. Ideally, you'd want your rental to be in a nice residential area where everyone else owned their own homes. That way you'd have the maximum benefits that come from "pride of ownership." Unfortunately, it's rarely the case that you'll be the only rental around. That's particularly so if you're purchasing a multifamily structure. Therefore, it's important to ask an agent what the mix of tenants to owners in the overall neighborhood is. Ideally it will be well below 15 percent. Anything with more than 20 to 25 percent tenants should be a warning flag. (Many lenders, for example, will refuse to offer financing in condo developments where there are more than 25 percent tenants.) Your agent may not know the exact answer,

but should be able to come up with a good approximation—or know whom to ask to get it. Of course, some
neighborhoods are made up entirely of multifamily rental
buildings. My own suggestion is that you stay away from
these. The crowding, noise, and competition usually
make them undesirable as investments.

Is it considered a "desirable community"?

Every agent knows which communities are desirable
and which aren't. However, agents are hesitant to simply
tell you because they could be accused of "steering":
leading you to or away from ethnic or racial areas. That's
a "no-no" for them. Nevertheless, it's important for you
to know if the area in which you're planning on investing
is "up and coming" or on the decline. Most (not all, see
below) investors look for the better areas. Therefore, I
would persist and ask about the subjects peripheral to
the question. For example, you might ask, "Are the owners in the area fixing up their properties?" Usually it's the
hotter areas where owners spend the money on improvement. Or, "Which areas are showing the most rapid price
appreciation?" Again, that almost defines a desirable
area. Or even, "If you were buying an investment property, which area would you pick   and why?" Keep in
mind that many investors have made fortunes by buying
cheaply in poorer, declining areas and then renting out
the properties ruthlessly. What makes an area desirable
as a home for you to live in may not be the same thing as
what makes an area desirable as a rental.

Is it part of your "farm"?

Most real estate agents "farm" certain neighborhoods. It's
a tried-and-true method of growing their business. Farming means that they go around a well-defined geographical area (typically a tract or development) several times a
year and introduce themselves to the owners. They knock
on doors, leave brochures, discuss the housing market,
and ask if anyone wants to sell (or buy). They also send
mailings out on a regular basis and sometimes make
phone calls to owners they've previously contacted. The
whole purpose is to get clients—mostly sellers, but sometimes buyers. What's important to you is that, in your

search for a good investment property, you want authoritative advice on the characteristics of an area. And if that area happens to be part of an agent's "farm," he or she is in a position to tell you everything about it. In fact, agents frequently know the floor plans of all the homes in the area, who built them, how good (or bad) the schools are, the crime rate, the prices, and even many of the owners. Ask about investment property within an agent's "farm," and you're likely to get all your questions answered quickly and accurately.

Is there a homeowners' association?

It's important to be aware of any homeowners' associations (HOAs) in an area where you're thinking of investing. While condominiums obviously have condominium associations, it's less apparent in single-family detached housing (SFDH). Yet some neighborhoods of SFDHs have strong HOAs. And these homeowner associations can play havoc with your plans to improve or change the property, as well as with your ability to rent to long-term tenants. This is not to say that the HOAs can prevent you from renting a property—normally they can't. But they can have strict rules that regulate such things as the color of the exterior, the type of roofing, the condition of landscaping, on-street parking, driveway parking, noise levels, number of occupants per unit, restrictions of tenants using common facilities such as a pool, tennis court, or club houses, and so on. Sometimes these rules are simply not legal. But short of taking the HOA to court, you probably will have to abide by them. Therefore, it's wise to find out in advance if your ownership will be crippled by a raft of rules that may have the consequence of impeding your ability to rent your property for a profit.

What is the income level of most tenants?

The lifeblood of most real estate investors is the tenant. The tenant is the one who provides you with the income to cover your mortgage payments, taxes, insurance, and, hopefully, repairs and maintenance. Good tenants are vital to your survival as a real estate entrepreneur. Therefore, you should check to see that the income level of your potential tenant matches that of the rent you'll need to charge. For example, if the tenant base is mostly high-income white collar and you are buying a rental home that you hope to rent out for $2,500 a month, you're probably in good shape. On the other hand, if your tenant base is mostly blue-collar low- to mid-income earners, then you could have trouble getting and keeping tenants. The same applies the other way around. A house that you intend to rent for $750 a month may simply neither impress nor attract high-income white collar workers. Most agents who've been in business in the area for at least five years will know what the tenant base is like. Be sure to look for an agent who has specialized in rental property, perhaps even owns several rentals himself or herself. Their insight into the rental market can be vitally important to you.

5

Will the Property Make a Suitable Rental?

QUESTIONS TO ASK YOURSELF

Are you ready to start in residential real estate?

☐

There are many ways to invest in real estate from commercial/industrial to bare land (see later chapters), from dealing in options to becoming a dealer in property. The one avenue most pursued by new investors, however, is to buy a home or condo, rent it out, and hold it while waiting for price appreciation to bring in the profits. If this is the course you have chosen and you have selected a house (or condo), you need to ask yourself if your choice is suitable as a rental. It's important to understand that not all homes make good rentals. Some are perfect for owner-occupants and some are perfect for tenants, but often the same home is not perfect for both.

Is the home too big/too small for tenants?

☐

The size of the home is critical in evaluating it for tenant use. If it's too small, you may have trouble renting it out. If it's too big, you may get too many people living in it, which will produce more wear and tear than you'll like. For example, a one- or two-bedroom single-family house isn't likely to appeal to tenants who have children. They will want more bedrooms. And since most tenants do have children, you'll be narrowing your pool of possible candidates. Most likely you'll have to find a single person or couple to rent to. That could mean a longer rent-up time. On the other hand, if you have a single-family house with five bedrooms, you're likely to appeal to very large families, those with many children. (You're also likely to appeal to two-family groups who want to share a place to save money on the rent.) While there's nothing wrong with lots of kids, they do tend to produce a lot of wear on the property. And don't think you can restrict the number of children in a rental. According to the Fair Housing Act of 1968, you cannot discriminate on the basis of familial status, which means children under the age of 18 living with parents or legal custodians. Indeed, it's very hard to limit the number of occupants in a house. Fire department regulations sometimes specify that a bedroom cannot be occupied by more than two adults and two children. That's 20 people in a five-bedroom house! All of which is to say: if you're looking for a rental, a big house will likely get you a very big family. Most investors prefer a home of three bedrooms and at least two baths. In some measure, getting just the right size applies also to condos and even to apartments (one to two bedrooms is usually ideal here).

Is the home too old to be a rental?

Few new investors think about the age of the property as an important consideration when buying for investment. But it is. While it's possible to rent out almost any property, it's simply a fact that older properties need far more maintenance and repair (M&R). Indeed, as homes get to be more than 10 years old, the amount of M&R increases dramatically. At more than 30 years of age, there's likely to be a hundredfold increase in the costs of M&R. Don't believe it? Consider. Short of defects (which in some cases may be covered under a builder's warranty), there's little likely to go wrong with a house during its first 10 years of life. Yes, there may be light bulbs to replace and filters to change, but most of the home's systems should operate flawlessly. However, starting at about year 11, things start to go wrong. In some areas with sediment or minerals in the water, the water heater can go out. That can easily be a $500 replacement bill. The house is also likely to need painting both inside and out, which can cost upwards of $4,000 to $5,000. Fences may need repairs, kitchens and baths may have broken tile or cabinets. In short, the repairs will start. By year 30, they could skyrocket. Depending on the type, the home might need a new roof. That could be anywhere from $8,000 to $25,000. A new heater and air conditioner could be in order—add another $5,000. In some areas of expansive soil, the foundation can crack. That could be $50,000 to fix it and any associated structural damage. And don't even think of homes that are historic—more than 100 years old. Termites could have eaten through much of the wood. The plumbing and electrical may need to be replaced. In short, the whole house might need to be revamped. All of which is to say that when looking for rental property, the newer the better.

Does the rental fit the job base?

In the last chapter we talked about the types of tenants you're likely to get in terms of white-collar workers and blue-collar workers. It's important that the home you select fits the type of tenant that's available. For example, if you're in an industrial area where most people work in a meat-packing plant for low- to mid-range wages, a small mid-priced three-bedroom/two-bath home is likely to appeal. There should be many tenants who can afford to rent the property. On the other hand, if you're in an area where there are many high-tech companies that pay very large salaries, the tenant base may turn up its nose at your mid-priced home. Rather, it's looking for something bigger and more elaborate. A home with lots of square footage with high-end features is more likely to appeal. Yes, you'll pay far more for such a house. But, on the other hand, you're likely to be able to rent it for more money and more quickly in its market. The point is that the rental should fit the job market. You don't want to have to wait months to rent up your property because it's too high-end or too low-end for the tenant base.

Is the lot too large?

Most first-time home occupant/buyers as well as first-time investors want a property with a big lot. It's very appealing. The idea is that there's "room to roam," as real estate agents sometimes describe it in their listings and advertising. You can plant fruit trees, garden, have a patio, a place to park an RV vehicle, even a pool and spa. The big yard harkens back to an earlier agricultural and rural era that many of us fondly think of as "the good old days." Unfortunately, the good old days (if they ever existed) have no place in a modern real estate rental. A large yard simply means more maintenance. Unless it's all cement (unlikely), there's going to be a lawn to water and mow. There will be shrubs to trim and fertilize, trees to tend, and so on. And the question quickly becomes "Who's going to do the work?" If you have a small lot, often the tenant will be agreeable to doing what minor maintenance there is. But, with a large lot, most tenants, even if they initially agree, soon discover that they'd rather spend their weekends having fun than spending them tending the landlord's yard. All of which means that in addition to paying for a large water bill (which you will want to pay for to ensure the yard is green), you'll also probably have to pay for a gardener. Yes, you might be able to eke out a few more dollars in rent for a house with a gardener, but nowhere near enough to justify the cost. In short, look for a rental house that has a small, not a large, lot.

Does it have a pool or spa?

Everyone wants a pool and a spa. No one wants to take care of them. If you buy a rental property that includes a pool and spa, chances are you may be able to get a small amount more in rent than you would for a similar property next door without those amenities. On the other hand, you'll need to hire a pool service to take constant care of your pool and spa. And chances are that will cost far more than your small increase in rent. Then there's the liability. If a tenant gets hurt or, God forbid, dies in your pool or spa, you can be sure you're going to be held financially liable. That means you'll want to carry heavy liability insurance—well into the millions of dollars. And for rentals with pools and spas, the premiums are steep. Of course, many investors figure they'll ask the tenant to take care of the pool/spa. After all, they're the ones enjoying it, aren't they? Yes, but don't count on tenants to maintain those amenities. They require constant testing of the water and adding proper chemicals, usually acid/base and chlorine. These are highly active chemicals and, if handled improperly by a tenant, can produce serious burns and other problems—another liability issue. Finally, there's the risk that the tenant may simply throw up his or her hands and stop tending the pool. If it's in a hot summer, in just a few weeks algae can develop and, depending on the type, quickly ruin an otherwise good pool. Acid washing costs several hundred dollars. If that doesn't work, replastering can cost $5,000 to $10,000. And that doesn't even add in the cost of replacing damaged filters, pumps, and heaters. In short, if you're looking for an investment rental, buy one *without* a pool and spa. The exception is if you're purchasing a large multifamily property. Tenants of big apartment buildings usually expect a pool/spa. Of course, with a large apartment building, you should be able to afford professional pool service, and you're going to carry heavy liability insurance coverage anyhow.

Is it close to my home?

We've already discussed this in the previous chapters, but it bears mentioning again. This actually should be the first question you ask yourself. If you've got 100 units, or even 20 units, you can easily afford to hire a property management firm to look after them. They typically charge 10 to 11 percent of the gross rentals to handle management and then bill out (to you) all costs for repairs and maintenance. On the other hand, if you only have one or two rentals, then you're the maintenance guy or gal. You simply won't be able to afford to hire someone else to do it. There's not going to be enough money. And that means that you'll have to be there when it's time to show the property to prospective tenants. You're on call when there's a leak and the tenant wants it fixed in the middle of the night. If you live in another state or across the country, are you going to hop on a plane each time there's an emergency or even a vacancy? If not, plan on spending lots of bucks hiring someone close by the rental to do it for you. On the other hand, if you're no more than 30 minutes away by car, you can indeed be a "Johnny on the spot." You can run out and show the property when it's for rent. You can spend a Saturday cleaning it up. If a faucet springs a leak, you can be there in short order to replace a 20-cent washer. It all hinges on how close you are to the rental. The closer the better (although being right next door can be a pain if the tenant constantly barrages you with requests). Look for rentals that are close by. Avoid those that are at a distance.

6
What's the Condition of the Property?

QUESTIONS TO ASK YOURSELF

☐

Do I understand how condition affects value?

Would you pay the same amount of money for a car that has a wrecked engine as you would for a car that is running? I think not. The same holds true for real estate. A property that's run down isn't worth nearly as much as one that's in top shape. That's why it's so important to determine the true condition of any real estate you're considering purchasing. In the residential market, professional home inspections have become the norm. That has always been the case for the commercial market—at least for savvy investors. Thus, no matter what type of property you're purchasing, you should get a determination of its true condition from someone who knows. That can be a professional inspector or, if you have an investment team, the person on your team who can best evaluate the physical condition of the property. Most times it's difficult to get an inspection done beforehand. This is especially the case with residential property since in a hot market there are likely to be many offers. You want to get yours in first. Therefore, be sure to include a contingency clause (a clause making the purchase subject to its conditions) that provides you with enough time *after* the sellers sign to do a thorough inspection. (Fourteen days is the most commonly used time frame.) Then, if you turn up something adverse, you can renegotiate your price downward to a more realistic offer. Don't remove your right to an inspection just because you want to beat some other buyer/investor to the punch. You might end up grossly overpaying for the property when you ultimately learn its true condition.

Can I inspect the property myself?

You certainly can if you're the buyer. Of course, the seller could always refuse to let you have an inspection. But, if that happens, you have to assume there's something seriously wrong that the seller wants to hide—an excellent reason for passing on the deal. You can go along with a professional inspector. And you can conduct your own informal inspection *prior* to making an offer, thus giving yourself a good opportunity to learn the true value of the property. Often you can do a quick check while previewing the property if the seller doesn't object. Keep in mind, however, that your personal inspection is only going to be as good as your knowledge of what to look for. If you're a structural engineer or used to be a building inspector who worked for the county, then your judgment should be excellent. But, if in your previous life you were an accountant, or a salesperson, or something else outside of the building industry, then chances are your inspection isn't going to reveal much. You simply won't know what to look for.

Should I have a professional inspection?

It's important that you put into the purchase agreement that you also have the right to designate a professional to do the inspection for you. Most professional home inspectors belong to national trade organizations such as ASHI (American Society of Home Inspectors), as well as local groups. Just be sure that when the inspector comes to take a look, you go along. No, you don't have to be an athlete to do this, but it can require some physical climbing around and it can be dirty, so know your physical limitations. By going along you can ask the inspector questions. You can point to areas that you are curious about. You may find your fears allayed or confirmed. You can often learn far more by listening to a good inspector's verbal comments than by reading a report. Many written reports contain so many caveats to protect the inspector that the information in them turns out to be bland and nearly useless.

Is there any plumbing distress?

You can quickly do a survey of any property's plumbing on your own. Of course, if you find anything (or the professional inspector does), then you'll want to call in a plumber to check it out and give you a bid on correcting the situation. I have a five-point plumbing check-up that I do:

1. Flush the toilets repeatedly. The water should go down as quickly after the last flush as the first. Any delay, particularly in later flushes, suggests a clogged sewer line. It could be as simple as sending a metal "snake" down to correct it for a few hundred dollars, or as complex as replacing a pipe clogged with tree roots for many thousands of dollars.

2. Look for sediment in the toilet bowls, sinks, and tubs. This indicates that the water has particles in it that can quickly clog up a water heater and ruin the washers in faucets.

3. Turn on all the faucets in the house at once while flushing the toilets. You may notice a decrease in pressure, but there still should be a good flow. If the water turns into a trickle, chances are the pipes are plugged (costing thousands to fix), or there's low water pressure coming to the house (about which there's little you can do).

4. Look for leaks. Particularly check under sinks and around the water heater. (A water heater costs about $500 to replace, unless it's led to black mold, which can cost thousands to remove.)

5. See if the pipes are cast iron, which was used in houses until the 1980s. It has a lifespan of 30 to 50 years, depending on the electrolytic character of the soil. Typically it will eventually rust through and spring high-pressure leaks. While a pressure pad can solve individual problems, usually the entire property must be replumbed in copper (costing $10,000 or more).

Is the electrical system in good shape?

As with plumbing, you can quickly do a survey of any property's electrical system on your own. Of course, if you find anything amiss (or the professional inspector

does), then you'll want to call in an electrician to check
it out and give you a bid on correcting the situation.
*Never work on any electrical appliance, wiring, or circuit
while the electricity is on.* Here are five things you can
check out:

1. Do all of the electrical appliances work? If not, is it just
    the appliance that's broken or is it the circuit? Usually
    you can tell because if a circuit is bad, several lights,
    plugs, and appliances will be down at the same time.

2. Are there GFI (ground fault interrupter) sockets in all
    bathrooms and kitchen areas? You can tell because
    they have keys you can push to test them. (Sometimes
    several plugs will be on one GFI circuit.) These are
    required in all modern housing and if you're using
    the property as a rental, you'll want them to be there.
    (Cost can be anywhere from a few hundred dollars to
    thousands to replace plugs, depending on whether
    the original wiring contains a ground wire, which is
    sometimes not found in older homes.)

3. Check the breaker panel. It's usually found either out-
    side or inside near the garage or sometimes in the
    basement. It should state the capacity. Two hundred
    amps is considered minimum in a modern house. It
    should also have circuit breakers. The old style was
    fuses. Replacing and upgrading a breaker panel can
    easily cost several thousand dollars.

4. Turn on all the lights in the house and then the air con-
    ditioning (if available). While there might be a
    momentary dimming of the lights, they should imme-
    diately return to full brightness. If the lights stay dim
    when all are turned on or when the air conditioning is
    turned on, the circuitry is inadequate and could lead
    to a short, which might start a fire. The potential lia-
    bility suggests you'll want to have the house rewired
    including a new breaker panel. (The cost could easily
    be $10,000 or more.)

5. Look at all of the wall plugs and turn on all of the
    switches. Any black, sooty areas around a wall plug
    suggest a short that momentarily caused a small fire.
    Any switches that don't work suggest a further prob-
    lem. Both indicate further inquiry by a professional.

Does the roof leak?

Roof repairs can be fairly inexpensive, costing in the hundreds of dollars. However, sometimes the entire roof must be replaced, which is one of the most costly things you can do to a house. Prices typically start at around $10,000 and go up from there. You should be suspicious of the roof of any house more than 10 years old. If the house is over 30 years old, you should assume there might be roof problems. If you see problems, or your professional inspector indicates there are some, have a roofer check it out. *Don't climb on the roof yourself. You could fall and be injured or killed. You could also damage certain types of roofs, such as tile.* There are three good ways you yourself can check the condition of the roof:

1. Look for stains on the ceiling or at the tops of walls. This is a giveaway that the roof leaks.

2. Look up into the attic on a sunny day. (You don't need to climb into the attic to do this. Be careful of falling or stepping through a ceiling if you climb into the attic.) If you can see pinpoints of light in a dark attic, it probably means you need a new roof. If there is light coming in at just one spot, a localized repair might be in order.

3. Go across the street from the house and look at the roof through a pair of binoculars. Check for missing, curled, or torn shingles. Look for flashing (the metal around chimneys and at valleys) that's discolored, broken, or in disarray.

Are any appliances worn out?

Kitchen appliances have a lifespan of more than 10 years. Sometimes they'll last 20 or even 30 years, but not often. When investing in residential real estate you need to consider appliances from two perspectives: the tenant's and the buyer's to whom you'll eventually resell. Unless you're buying a very up-scale property, most tenants won't really care how modern the appliances are, just that they work. Consequently, buying a property with older appliances isn't necessarily a bad thing for long-term investment. The tenants will be able to use the older appliances and you can replace them as they wear out. The cost for basic models, including installation, is roughly:

Garbage disposal:	$150
Electric stove/oven:	$600
Dishwasher:	$550
Refrigerator:	$600 (tenants usually bring their own refrigerators)

On the other hand, if you plan to resell the property within the next five years and hope to get top dollars, you may want to replace all of the older appliances with newer and more up-scale models. The cost can easily be $5,000. Remember, in a resale it's not just a matter of whether or not the appliance works. It's also a matter of how modern and elegant it looks. And that adds considerably to cost.

Do I need to remodel kitchen or bath?

So long as everything works, most tenants will put up with old-fashioned tile, linoleum, and plastic countertops. They won't really care that much if the cabinets are nicked and scratched a bit. In short, because it isn't their property, tenants don't expect everything to be perfect. (An exception is if you're renting out a high-end property. Tenants paying many thousands a month in rent look for near perfection in the property.) On the other hand, if you're planning on selling within five years, you may find you'll get a quicker sale for far more money than you put in by upgrading the kitchen and at least the master bathroom. It's important to understand that a modern kitchen or bath with new cabinets, a stone countertop, tile floors, and so on add immensely to the value of the property. Most homeowners, however, rarely recoup their investment because they buy the highest quality fixtures at the highest price. It is possible to get inexpensive new "starter line" cabinets for less than half the cost of the top-of-the-line models. Similarly, depending on how you handle edges and back splashes (inexpensive tile will often do very well), you can get a granite countertop for a fraction of the price a homeowner will pay. In short, by being judicious in your remodeling, you can redo a kitchen or bath for $15,000 instead of the $50,000 it might cost a homeowner and recoup all of the money invested *plus* get more for the home and a quicker sale. Note: Remodeling only makes sense when the home is older and the existing kitchen/baths are substantially out of date or of poor quality.

Are there any cracks in the foundation?

Obviously the foundation is what holds up the house. If something's wrong with the foundation, the whole house could be affected. It might not tumble down, but floors could be at weird angles, doors could jam, windows not open, the roof sag, and potentially dangerous structural problems occur. It behooves you to know whether or not the property you are buying has a foundation problem. (You might still want to buy even with a problem, if you can get it cheap enough and have a plan for correcting it.) You can examine the foundation yourself and usually get a pretty good idea of its condition. Simply walk around the structure, keeping about 5 feet away. Look at the cement (or bricks) between the dirt and the start of the building. You're looking for anything unusual. (Note: Be sure you get the seller's permission to pull back bushes so you can get a clean view.) If you spot something, get a professional in there to check it out. There are three most revealing problems:

1. *Cracks.* Small cracks (those less than one thirty-second of an inch wide) are common in concrete and don't usually signify a problem. Wider cracks, particularly "V" shaped ones that are wider at the top than the bottom suggest a very serious problem.

2. *Offsets.* Here the concrete is cracked and the edges no longer meet. One section may be sagging or they may be off horizontally with one part protruding. Again, this suggests a very serious problem.

3. *Erosion.* Sometimes the ground will erode from around and even underneath the foundation. Without the support of the earth, the foundation is vulnerable and might soon crack or break. This can often be fixed by replacing the missing dirt and compacting it.

Sometimes sellers will try to conceal serious foundation problems by filling in cracks or offsets with new concrete and painting over all of it. Unscrupulous sellers will then not disclose the problem. Usually, however, if you look very closely, you can detect this sort of work . . . but not always.

Is there any water damage?

Water is the bane of structures. In expansive soil it can cause foundations and slabs to distort and break. Standing in basements, it can cause moisture and mold damage. Freezing in foundations and pools, it can cause breaks and cracks. Running off, it can remove supporting soil. It's important to check to see if water has caused problems in the past, because if it has, it will likely cause even more problems in the future. Here are five quick checks for water damage:

1. Does the ground slope into or away from the structure? Ideally, the ground will slope away, making sure that all water runs away from the structure. Ground sloping inward can cause standing water that can ruin a foundation. It can sometimes be corrected simply by re-grading.

2. In the basement (if there is one) is there a water line on the cement wall? While it might currently be the dry season, this will indicate flooding during the wet season. Flooding of a basement can cause damage to a foundation as well as the formation of mold. Sometimes re-grading outside will solve the problem. Other times a sump pump must be installed to remove water as it appears.

3. Are all gutters and drain spouts in good order? Most people think these are designed to keep them from getting wet when it rains. Actually they are designed to catch water and direct it away from the structure. Repairing gutters and drains is usually inexpensive. Replacing them can cost thousands of dollars.

4. Are there any sink holes in the yard? These are easy to spot in wet weather because they are characterized by pools of standing water. In dry weather, you have to use your eye to judge. (If sellers permit, you can

attempt to flood an area with a garden hose to see if water pools.) This can cause damage to landscaping and, if it leads into the basement, damage to the structure. Correction may involve digging trenches and installing "French drains" to lead the water away. Again, the price is usually in the thousands of dollars.

5. Are there any leaning fences? Fences are very susceptible to water damage. Water can rot away the underpinnings of wood and cause brick and cement walls to topple over. Leaning fences are a red flag that there might be serious water problems with the property. Have a soil engineer check it out.

Is there insulation?

All modern homes and office, commercial, and industrial buildings are built with heavy insulation. This is done in large part to reduce the cost of heating and cooling these structures. However, 50 years ago little insulation was used in buildings. Back then, few structures had air conditioning and the cost of gas/oil to heat buildings was minuscule compared to today. If you're buying a building that's more than 20 years old, you should check to see that it has adequate insulation. ("Adequate" is determined by the weather in your area. In freezing winters and burning summers, R-34 in ceilings and R-19 in walls and floors are usually required. In more moderate climates, R-19 in ceilings and R-11 in walls are typically used.) While you may not be worrying too much because the tenants will be paying the electric and gas/oil bills, you may find your turnover rate higher than expected as the tenants move out to buildings that have better insulation. By the way, adding insulation (except for blowing it into attics) after a building is completed is usually prohibitively expensive. Further, when it's time to resell, you can be sure the next buyer will be looking at the insulation of the building. Today, with the high cost of utilities, it's a big issue for residential as well as commercial tenants. If the insulation is low or missing entirely, you can expect to have a harder time selling and expect to receive lower bids. You can check for insulation most easily by looking in the attic. To check in the walls, *turn off the electricity*, remove a cover plate from a plug or switches, and carefully poke around the edges of it (without damaging the wall) into the inner wall area. You should quickly be able to determine if there's insulation in the walls.

Is there lead paint?

You can assume that any residential building constructed prior to 1978 will have some lead paint in it. That's the year lead paint was banned in residential property. (It's not as big an issue in commercial real estate.) Your home seller is required by federal law to give you, as a buyer, a lead paint disclosure, a booklet on the hazards of lead paint, and a 10-day period in which you can investigate the property for lead paint and either modify the purchase agreement or back out of the deal if it's found. As a landlord, you are likewise required to present a disclosure on lead paint to your tenants. (You're not required to investigate or mitigate.) However, it's almost impossible during a casual inspection for you or a professional inspector to determine if the house has lead paint. What's required is to take samples and ship them off to a lab for analysis. This can take a week or longer and can cost several hundred dollars. (Check with www.epa.gov for approved labs.) If there's lead paint in the home, it can chip, flake, or dust off and contaminate food and air where it can cause a host of illnesses. Children are particularly at risk, especially so since some will gnaw on windowsills and door molding, thus ingesting the lead. As a landlord, you may have liability issues with lead paint. The biggest problem is the difficulty in removing the lead paint. Sanding, burning, and scraping can cause it to be released into the air. The most common method is to simply remove the boards it's on and have them shipped to a toxic waste site for disposal—an expensive procedure. The lead paint issue is a big concern for investors buying rental residential property. For more information check into the Web site noted above.

Are there asbestos hazards?

Asbestos is also a major hazard in homes and commercial and industrial buildings. It can cause lung disease and a variety of other illnesses. However, as of this writing there are no federal rules requiring disclosure of asbestos in residential property. It can be found in myriad products, including floor and ceiling tiles, "popcorn" or blown-in ceilings, insulation around ducts and hot appliances, and more. Generally its use has been greatly reduced since 1978. Asbestos is a flaky white material, but it is almost impossible to identify it definitively short of a laboratory examination. The greatest danger from asbestos usually comes when it is disturbed, for example, a heating pipe with asbestos insulation around it is damaged, releasing the asbestos into the atmosphere. Correction usually involves either removing the asbestos or encapsulating. It cannot be done by the average person. Rather, for safety reasons, it must be done by an asbestos mitigation company and the cost can be enormous.

Is there any black mold?

Black mold has probably been around for far longer than people. Black mold has long been reported to cause minor illnesses, especially allergies. Allegations now abound, however, that it can cause *severe* illness or even death. In the last few years, the hysteria surrounding having it in the home has reached amazing proportions. Owners and tenants have moved out of homes and refused to move back in when black mold was discovered. Tenants of commercial and industrial buildings have demanded owners/landlords have the black mold removed as a condition for continued leasing of the property. And, in some well publicized cases, insurance companies have paid out hefty amounts to have houses almost rebuilt to remove the black mold as well as paying significant awards to owners. Today, in real estate you don't want to get caught buying a building, whether to live in or rent, that has black mold. If a structure does have it, you want to insist that the owner/seller pay to have it removed. Chances are you may not be able to get hazard insurance coverage on a building that has had black mold. While it takes an expert to identify it, you can usually spot it yourself. It requires moisture to live and grow, hence is most commonly found in kitchens, baths, and utility rooms. Look in cabinets and under sinks. Usually it will be where there are leaks. It generally appears exactly as its name suggests—it is mold that's black. A pest inspection company (termite company) can normally positively identify and give a quote for removing it. By the way, if you buy a property that's significantly reduced in price because of black mold, remember, you'll have to pay to have it removed . . . or resell at a discount yourself later on.

Does the furnace work?

Be sure the property has a furnace or other heating system. (Not all do!) Regardless of the time of year, turn the furnace or heating system on. Put your hand to vents or radiators to make sure heat is coming out. The worst thing is to get a call at the beginning of winter from a tenant complaining there's no heat. Then, on an emergency basis to calm the tenant, you might have to install a new and expensive (often costing many thousands of dollars) heating system. If discovered prior to purchase, you can have the seller pay for it. Note: Sometimes heaters will work, but may be dangerously defective. For example, a forced air furnace uses a heat exchanger to transfer the heat from burning gas to the air in the structure. If it has leaks, even pinhole ones, it could release toxic fumes into the air, thus poisoning tenants. A good professional inspector or a gas company representative can usually determine if the heat exchanger is defective. Typically, it's cheaper to buy a new furnace than to replace the part. The cost is upwards of $2,500 in a residential property.

Is there hot water?

It's a good idea to inspect the property when the gas and electricity are turned on. That way you can check to see that there's hot water. Simply turn on the hot water faucet in any bathroom, kitchen, or utility room and wait. After a short time, very hot water should be coming out. If there's no hot water, or it's only lukewarm, it could be a defective water heater. Have a plumber check it out. Also, check the size of the water heater. Today, 50 gallons is considered adequate for an average-sized home. In an office building with a couple of bathrooms, a 30-gallon heater might be required. Keep in mind that, as with most things, water heaters have improved over time. Today's new heaters are capable of "stirring" up the water to help prevent sediment from forming. (Sediment is the biggest cause of water heater failure. It builds up in the bottom of the tank and causes increased wear on the metal at the same time as reducing the temperature of the water.)

Does the air conditioning work?

Today, central air conditioning is standard in virtually all areas of the country. Only in certain coastal areas where the temperature is moderate most of the year is it not found. It costs around $3,000 to completely replace a central air-conditioning system in the average sized home. The cost can be far more for an industrial or commercial unit. While air conditioners can be serviced, that usually just means checking out the filter and being sure the unit has a full charge of gas. Mostly, they go without much care until they break. If the property you're considering has air conditioning, you should turn it on to be sure it works. The air coming from vents should immediately be cooler. You can ask your professional inspector to measure it. This is done by placing a thermometer in the return (where it goes into the unit) and another at the most distant register (where it comes out). The drop in temperature should be at least 10 degrees. Anything less and the unit will have trouble cooling the building. Note: Sometimes air conditioning units are simply too small. If that's the case, they'll work constantly, cost a lot in electricity, and never cool properly. They might need to be replaced, even though they're not broken. Also, consider any air conditioning unit over 10 years old likely to need replacement soon.

Is there a temperature/relief valve on the water heater?

This comes under the heading of safety. A temperature/relief valve is designed to vent steam and hot water from a water heater when the internal pressure goes too high. This prevents what can be a devastating explosion. (In the past, whole buildings have been flattened when a water heater blew.) The valve is usually near the top. You can check it by opening it and allowing some water to drain. (Sometimes with very old valves, when opened, the rust inside will keep them from closing, meaning you'll have to replace it!) It's usually around $100 to have a plumber replace the valve. If one isn't present, you'll want it installed to reduce liability and bring the water heater up to code. Installation shouldn't cost more than $250.

Is the water heater strapped?

Another concern in areas subject to hurricanes, tornados, and earthquakes is that the water heater be securely strapped to the structure. This is to prevent it from falling over during the movement of the earth or the building. When a water heater falls over, it often ruptures the lines attached to it. This not only means water getting all over everything, but the shorting out of electrical wires or the creation of gas leaks. Houses have burnt down because a heavy water heater tipped. Strapping can be done by a handyman or a plumber. Sometimes building supply stores will offer the service. It's usually not more than a couple of hundred dollars. Ask your professional inspector to check that the water heater in question is properly strapped.

Are there any nonpermitted additions?

Owners/sellers will often add to their properties without the benefit of building permits. There are many reasons they might do this: Permits are expensive and inspectors often demand inconvenient and costly changes; the owners/sellers may not have realized it was necessary; the owners/sellers did the work themselves; and so on. There are many problems in buying property with nonpermitted (NP) additions. One is liability. If tenants are injured in a NP addition, they might sue the owner (which could be you), claiming that faulty workmanship caused their injuries. If the local building department learns of the NP work, it could demand it be brought up to code or torn down. (Don't make the mistake of thinking you can easily bring NP work up to code. Permitted work is inspected several times in the building process, and often it's easier to tear out NP work and start over than to try to get an inspector to approve an NP job.) Finally, when you go to resell, you'll need to disclose that the property has an NP addition, and this will impinge on your getting the highest price. You can often tell an addition because, no matter how well done, it may not quite blend in with the rest of the structure. Alcoves, doors in strange places, a break in the flooring or ceiling are all giveaways. Be sure to ask the owner/seller for a copy of the permit if you discover an addition. If it's NP, you may want to nix the deal, demand a lower price, or ask that the owner get it permitted.

Are there any odors?

This is a tricky one, yet it can be a real problem for investors. Many times homes and larger buildings have odors. They can come from old cooking, poor drainage vents in the plumbing, moisture under the carpeting, mold, pets, and a hundred other sources. Often odors are transitory and not serious. But sometimes, they can be very serious and costly. Probably the worst are urine smells from pets, especially cats. If these are in a carpet, you can pretty much figure you'll have to replace the carpet, the padding, and perhaps even some of the flooring underneath! I've encountered them many times and tried many remedies, none of which seems to work. The only sure way to remove these smells from carpets is replacement. Of course, the key is knowing that the smells are there. If you tour the property on a day when the windows are all open and a breeze is blowing, you might not notice the smell. Before making a purchase some savvy investors will get right down on their hands and knees and sniff all around looking for pet odors! Keep in mind that it can easily cost $7,000 or more to recarpet the average size house. Other odors can often be removed by eliminating their source. Sometimes it's rotting food fallen behind a cabinet, other times it's items that have gotten wet from a leak and produced mold (see the question on black mold above). If you detect odors in a home, be sure you track down the source and the cost to remove them before completing a purchase.

Are there any "bad" neighbors?

For rental properties, neighbors are not usually a problem. Unless they're really bad neighbors! Some neighbors are simply pugnacious; they're always spoiling for a fight. It might be about over watering a lawn, or the home's color, or the tenants' children, or just anything. The last thing you want is to be losing tenants because of fights (both physical and emotional) that the neighbors are instigating. Thus, it's a good idea to ask the seller/owner about the neighbors. And if it's a clear bill of health, get it in writing. Also, check for complaints to the police department from the last tenant/owner regarding neighbors. These are kept on file and can usually be accessed (although the name of the person who lodged the complaint may not be available).

Do I have all previous and current reports?

Unless the property's brand new (and many times even if it is), there are going to be reports on it. Every time it previously sold, surely a professional inspection report was issued, as was a termite clearance and, depending on the area, seismic, flood, and other reports. You should get these reports and examine them. If nothing else, you can compare them to your own reports and they can tell you what changes have occurred to the property since they were issued. Many times old reports will bring to light problems that were glossed over by the seller. Ask the seller for copies. If the seller says they were lost, or there were none, get it in writing. If something later turns up, you want to be able to show that the seller was concealing it. Of course, you yourself will want to get appropriate new reports on the subject property. Your agent can help you determine what's usual in your area. For example, the property might be in a location where radon gas emissions are common. A radon report would be in order.

QUESTIONS TO ASK A PROFESSIONAL INSPECTOR

Can I accompany you on the inspection?

You certainly should be able to. After all, you're paying for it! However, some inspectors will refuse to let buyers accompany them. They may cite liability issues, such as if you fall and get hurt, or other concerns. My own feeling is that if an inspector refuses to let you go along, get a new inspector. One of the best ways to learn about a new property is to accompany a professional as he or she tours the property. The inspector will visit areas that you may never see. He or she will also be poking the foundation with a screwdriver, crawling under the house, scratching beams to check for dry rot, and hundreds of other things.

As soon as something is found, you can ask the nature of the problem, whether or not it's serious, and how it can likely be corrected (as well as for how much!). Further, you should have received the buyer's disclosures before you have the inspection. Thus, you can ask the inspector to check out anything that was disclosed. For example, the seller discloses that some of the floor joists are out of alignment. You and the inspector get under the house and see that the reason is that several have rotted through and need to be replaced. A small disclosure can sometimes lead to a big problem when investigated. Keep in mind, however, that inspectors sometimes go into hazardous areas. You'll need to be in fairly good shape to keep up and you should wear old, scruffy clothes because you could get dirty. Be careful when you're on the inspection. Carelessness could lead to a fall or some injury. Finally, keep in mind that virtually all inspections contain the caveat that they only cover accessible areas. The inspector won't look inside walls or under carpets. (Although, with a seller/owner's permission, the inspector may pull back a piece of the carpet to get a look at the flooring beneath.)

Is the roof in good shape?

This is something you're going to be particularly concerned about if you saw problems with the shingles or light shining through as noted above. The inspector may climb on the roof to check it out. (Don't go up yourself—it's too dangerous!) Or, he or she may say that you need to get a roofer. If that's the case, immediately call in the roofer. If possible, find someone who does roof inspections, but does not do reroofing or repairs. The reason is that a regular roofing contractor will simply come out and give you a bid on a new roof. Or he or she will come up with a complete fix for leaks in the roof. What you want, however, is a professional to tell you what, if anything, is wrong with the roof and to suggest a variety of treatments to correct the problem. Remember, a very old roof will probably need to be fully replaced, even if it's only got one leak (because others will soon be on the way). On the other hand, a new roof can probably be patched (at a fraction of the replacement cost), even it has half a dozen leaks.

How's the foundation?

While you examined the foundation by walking along the outside of the building (see above), you can expect the inspector not only to duplicate that, but also to go inside and look at it from under the house. (Remember, the inspection only looks at accessible areas. If there's no interior access to the foundation, it won't be examined.) Ask the inspector about any cracks you see. Also, get an explanation for offsetting. At the same time, watermarks should be explained, as should fluorescence, which is a kind of white material that sometimes comes off concrete that's been exposed to water. The inspector can be expected to poke and prod the concrete to tell you if there are rebars in it (reinforcing steel bars). These are put in at the time the foundation is poured and help hold it together, even when there are major cracks. Some houses, however, were built without rebars, and hence, any cracking of the foundation can lead to major separations and ultimately, the collapse of the building. Finally, the inspector should give you an opinion as to the aging of the concrete. A good cement mixture will last almost indefinitely. However, if there was too much or too little water when it was originally poured, it could deteriorate over time. Sometimes foundations that were poured badly simply crumble into dust as the decades go by.

How's the structure?

Most homes and buildings are wood structures. Metal framed buildings for residential use have only come into vogue in the last few years. Depending on how well the structure was built and what's happened to it over time (ground movement, falling trees, termites, and so on), it could be in anything from terrible to great shape. A good professional inspector should be able to give you an estimate of the structure's condition, even without being able to see into the walls. The reason is that with structures, problems get reflected and mirrored to other areas. For example, if there's a joist that wasn't properly connected, or that became separated, you should see significant cracking in the wallboards—a telltale sign. Of course, not all cracks are important. The diagonal cracks that sometimes go up from doorjambs and windows can simply indicate the normal settling of a house over time. On the other hand, straight vertical or horizontal lines may indicate a structural problem underneath. The inspector may also be able to actually see the structure in the attic, basement, garage, and other accessible areas. If so, a good inspector will be able to tell you if the joisting and beams are adequate, the boards in good shape, and if there are any other obvious problems. Be sure, however, that your inspector knows what he or she is talking about. I was once a seller when the buyer's inspector noted metal braces on floor posts under the house. His conclusion was that the posts were weak and damaged and it would cost thousands to repair them. The truth was that it was earthquake preventative work and no correction was necessary. Your inspection is only as good as your inspector.

What's the condition of the soil/water?

The typical home inspector is not going to be able to give you a soil report. For that, you need a soil engineering firm. However, if the home inspector notes a problem, you can then call out the soil engineer. Problems that inspectors look for are sinkholes, standing water, overly expansive soil, rock or pan close to the surface, and so on. Poor grading (for example, from the front of the lot to the rear instead of the other way around) is also usually spotted. Expect your professional inspector to recommend removing any debris from the side of the home that prevents water from running off to the street. Many times innocuous piles of rubbish left at the side prevent water runoff and cause standing puddles and these can result in damage to the foundation.

Are there any problems with the home's systems?

You've probably checked some of this out yourself as noted above. The inspector, however, can check every electrical plug to see that it's properly grounded and every switch to see that it functions correctly. He or she can check the circuit breakers as well as main grounds. The inspector will also check for leaks in the plumbing (only in accessible areas, however) as well as water pressure (you should be told the exact water pressure to the house as well as inside it), any leaking or damaged faucets, toilets, showers, and tubs. The inspector should also check out the heat exchanger on the furnace as well as the air conditioning system. In short, a good inspection will give you a thorough report on all of the home's systems, telling you which are in good shape, which have problems, and possibly even what can be done (as well as how much it will cost) to fix them.

Are there any mold problems?

As noted earlier, mold is today's big scary real estate bugaboo. That's not to say that there aren't serious issues with mold. However, in this author's opinion, the whole issue has been blown out of proportion. Nevertheless, if mold can be identified, it must be dealt with one way or another, even if that means bringing in the people in the bubble-suits. A good home inspector will search diligently for mold. It's usually going to be spotted in the kitchen and bathrooms in cabinets under sinks, around toilets, showers, and tubs, as well as in utility rooms. Sometimes, however, it grows in basements, attics, and even in walls. The one condition that seems necessary for its growth is moisture. If there's moisture in the property, you can almost bet there's going to be mold. If the inspector finds mold, then as an investor you should be sure to have the seller pay for its removal. Next to lead, black mold removal can be the most expensive hazardous material to remove. Getting rid of it and repairing the damage it caused can easily run into the tens of thousands of dollars. Also, be aware that if a claim has been made to an insurance company for black mold (most insurers no longer cover it) by the current owner/seller, you might have trouble getting hazard insurance yourself! Today a home's claim record travels with it and can affect not only the cost of insurance, but insurability itself.

How's the well?

Many properties don't have municipal water systems but rely on their own well water. If that's the case, you should have the well water analyzed. Look for fecal material and dangerous chemicals (such as arsenic) in the water. Fecal material usually occurs when the property has both a well and a septic tank system and there's cross contamination. A cure can be difficult as there's often not enough room to separate the septic tank and its leach field from the well. A property with a serious water well problem might be a good one to pass on.

Are there any environmental hazards?

These can include anything from a toxic waste dump site next door to asbestos, formaldehyde, radon gas, lead in paint and in water supplies to a dozen other hazards. A good professional inspector is trained to look for all of them and the clues they leave. A good inspector will also know the area and recommend further testing just to be sure there isn't a problem with the subject house. For example, if the area is known to have "blue water" (a condition where copper leaches out of pipes into the water system), he or she will tell you to have your water tested. In an area where radon gas is common, testing of the home's air supply should be suggested. In short, the inspector is your first line of defense against environmental hazards after the seller's disclosures and your own inspection.

Are there other problems I should know about?

This is a catch-all question that you should ask your inspector not only at the end of the inspection, but also at any junctures along the way. For example, you inspect the basement and are discussing problems that were found. Then there's a pause in the conversation as the inspector prepares to look elsewhere, and you ask, "Any other problems with the basement?" The inspector pauses and then says, "Now that you ask, there was a lot of oil on the floor under the oil storage tank. You might want to have it checked out for leaks." Ask the same question after inspecting the attic, the interior of the house, and any other areas. Remember, you're paying to learn about problems. One way to get your money's worth is to ask all you can.

7

Do You Know the Property's True Value?

QUESTIONS TO ASK YOURSELF

Are there comps?

One of the quickest and surest ways to determine value in real estate is to look at comparable sales (comps). This is especially the case in residential property. (We'll cover other types of property below.) The principle is simple to understand. If a house that's comparable in most ways to yours sold for $500,000, then chances are yours is worth close to that amount too. It's a good idea to examine at least three to five comps to get a good sense of the local market. Of course, there are many concerns with using comps as an appraisal tool. These include the timeliness of the comps, their true similarity, even the reliability of reported prices. We'll also look at these in the next questions. But first, it's important to understand that not all properties have comps. If the house you're considering purchasing is in a tract of hundreds of similar homes, than finding comps should be no problem. With condos and co-ops, finding comps is also usually no problem. But if you're considering a unique home (for example, one that was custom built), then finding comps can be difficult. This is particularly the case in higher-priced and rural areas. And when nearby comps aren't readily available, they can throw off the appraisal process. For example, when professional appraisers can't find nearby comparable homes, they sometimes will go to a distant location, perhaps dozens of miles away, where a similar home might have sold. They will extrapolate from that sale to the subject house. However, since all real estate is local, what homes in one area are selling for may have no bearing whatsoever on what homes in another area are selling for. If there are no comps in the immediate area, you should consider alternate methods of appraisal such as square foot cost, replacement cost, and capitalization of income (all discussed below).

Are the comps recent?

For the comps to be useful, they must be recent. How recent really depends on market trends. If the market has been slow moving, prices changing only a few percent a year, then a comp that's a year old may be fine to use. On the other hand, if the market is rapidly accelerating, as has been the case in recent years, then comps that are even six months old might be considered out of date. You might want to strive to get only comps that are from the most recent sales. Beware of real estate agents who go to their computers and pop out a dozen comps for the subject property and want you to use them for comparison when shopping. Check the dates. These older comps can lead to your making offers that are too low or too high depending on market trends. As a result, you'll miss out on getting a property for a good price.

Have I forward priced the comps?

It's important to remember that no matter how recent the comps may be, they are always going to be slightly out of date. The reason is that they reflect where prices were when the comparable properties were sold, not where they are today. However, sales prices are seldom released until after the deal has closed. (This is to protect the seller, who might have discounted the sale, from a new buyer who comes in after the sale has fallen through and now wants the discounted sales price.) This typically takes a minimum of 30 days, sometimes longer. Further, you may not find any very recent sales, so you could be relying on property that was sold up to six months (or more) ago. During that time span, the market may have changed significantly. For example, if the market is going up 12 percent a year, in six months it's presumably gone up 6 percent (half a year's worth). Thus, a comp from six months ago should be adjusted upward by 6 percent to reflect today's true price. (If the market is declining, the same principle applies.) This is called *forward pricing*. It's adjusting comp prices to the current market. It works both when the market's going up and when it's going down. Failure to make this adjustment is what often leads sellers to offer their homes for less (or more) than they're worth. A buyer who has forward priced the comps may see such a seller's error—and obtain a bargain price.

Are the comps truly similar?

You want to compare apples with apples, not with oranges. Even in a tract setting, there may be many different models with different floor plans, square footage, and amenities. Therefore, it's important to scrutinize the comps and to make adjustments where possible. For example, your home has a swimming pool, but comp homes do not. Obviously your home is worth more because of the pool. (Don't make the mistake of adding in the price of putting in a pool—the added value may be only 20 to 25 percent of the cost of putting in a new pool.) You should subtract from the price when the comps have more amenities or are better in some way and add to the price when your home has more amenities and is somehow better. Homes that have been upgraded, even if they are the same model as yours, will command significantly more than a house that has not been upgraded . . . and vice versa. What should become quite obvious is that this is an approximation game, not one with scientifically verifiable information. Nevertheless, as agents will confirm, after a while you get a feeling for the neighborhood and the comps and can come quite close to accurately appraising a house. Many agents who farm areas (*farming* means getting to know a neighborhood and regularly soliciting listings there) can often pinpoint the right price for a house just by walking through quickly. A savvy investor should develop the same skill.

Can I rely on the comp price?

Are the prices announced in the MLS (Multiple Listing Service) the actual prices received by sellers for the homes? Or have they been changed or manipulated in some way? Generally speaking, I've found that the reported prices tend to be highly accurate, especially today when financing is critical and the sales amount determines the mortgage size. However, keep in mind that there is often a significant difference between *sales* price and *asking* price. In a normal, calm market the sales price is typically between 5 to 10 percent lower than asking price. In a hot market, the sales price might actually be higher than the asking price! And in a cold market, the discount might be far greater. It can be helpful when trying to appraise a property to check out other homes listed nearby. Just keep in mind, however, that their asking prices may be far off what they actually will sell for once a buyer who is ready, willing, and able appears.

What is the GIM (gross income multiplier)?

There are many different ways of determining value in real estate. The GIM is one that is important when you are purchasing multi-unit residential as well as commercial property. Basically, it's a kind of shorthand or rule of thumb for quickly finding a price that many investors find quite helpful. Its use couldn't be simpler. You take the income from all sources for the property (building rents, parking rents, vending machines, and so forth) each month and annualize them (multiply by 12). Then you multiply the result by a multiplier that is a number that investors use in the current market. For example, if the gross income comes to $200,000 and the multiplier is 14, the property would be worth $2.8 million. Of course, I'm sure that careful readers are wondering where I got the multiplier from. While obtaining the gross annualized income should be fairly straightforward (check with the seller and the tenants), obtaining the multiplier can be a slightly more difficult task. The simplest way to obtain the multiplier is to ask. Real estate agents who deal in the type of property you're considering should have it on the tip of their tongues. So should other investors. Keep in mind, however, that the multiplier changes with market conditions. (It's actually obtained by going through the tedious process of comparing dozens of comps for similar properties, comparing price to annual gross income, and coming up with an average number.) While the GIM is a very useful quick tool, I wouldn't use it exclusively. I'd use several different approaches to determining value.

What is the capitalization of the net income?

This is a traditional method of determining the value of an income-producing property. What it essentially does is base the value on the amount of return you expect. To use it you determine the net income. This is the amount of money the property returns annually after all expenses are paid, excepting mortgage payments. For example, a property might produce $200,000 in gross income. However, after repairs, maintenance, and other costs that figure might be down to $150,000. Now, if you want to earn 10 percent on your money, you would divide that $150,000 by 10 percent and come up with $1,500,000. This essentially means that if you put $1.5 million into the property, you'll earn 10 percent on your money. If you want to earn 5 percent, you'll divide by 5 percent and find that you can afford to pay $3 million for the property. Of course, this assumes that you're paying all cash. Factoring in mortgage payments might mean that instead of getting any income at all, you'll have a negative cash flow situation in which it is costing you money out of your own pocket to maintain the property. Nevertheless, this method is very helpful when determining the rate of return on a property.

What is the square foot price?

Yet another way to determine price when buying multiunit residential, office, and industrial buildings is to check out the square foot price. For example, if property in the area is selling for $200 a square foot and your building has 10,000 square feet, the price might be $2,000,000. As with the GIM noted above, you should check with agents and other investors for what the current square foot price happens to be for this type of property in your area. Yet another measurement is the rental rate as determined by square footage. This is especially helpful in terms of office buildings. For example, one building might produce monthly rental income of $5 a square foot while another might produce income of $15 a square foot. It doesn't take a genius to see that the second building should be worth three times as much as the first, on a square footage basis.

What is the front foot price?

Sometimes when evaluating commercial property, particularly when it is located in a mall or on a heavily trafficked street, the price will most easily be determined by the *front foot*. This refers to the number of linear feet that the property has on the street (or mall walkway). It only stands to reason, since the ability of the property to generate income for the tenant may be determined, to a large degree, by the number of people who either walk or drive by. The more front footage, the more valued the property. For example, if the property has 100 front feet and the value per front foot is $15,000, the property may be worth $1,500,000. Note: The cost per front foot varies enormously, depending on the location. On a side street it could be a quarter of the cost of being on a main street. In addition, many businesses no longer rely on frontage to appeal to customers. Rather, signage, online advertising, even word of mouth can make an apparently poor location quite valuable. Further, front foot price is usually derived from rent. The property, for example, rents out for so much a front foot. When this is the case, annualizing the rents and then using a GIM can often work more effectively. To find the front foot value of a property, you should check with agents and other investors who deal in that type of property.

What is the replacement value?

Here we determine value based on how much it would cost to replace a property. While this is particularly useful when the property is brand new, it becomes decreasingly useful as the property ages. It's typically done by separating the value for the land from the cost of the building. For example, the lot a house is on might cost $600,000. (This figure should be obtained by checking comps for similar lots, if any are available.) The house, on the other hand, might cost $350,000 to replace if built from scratch. Thus the combined value of house and lot might be $950,000. For a just-completed house, this can be quite accurate, since that's probably very close to how much it would cost to replace this house on another similar lot. (Remember, the value of a new property usually is determined by the combined value of the lot and the house on it.) For an older house, the technique is less accurate. The reason is that it becomes difficult to accurately estimate replacement cost. (Bare lot cost, on the other hand, can usually be determined quite accurately.) The reason is that as homes grow older, they also grow increasingly obsolete. A home that's 25 years old, for example, is likely to have out-of-date bathrooms and kitchen as well as out-of-date windows (single pane), insulation (not enough), heating/air (too expensive to run), and so on. Thus, the replacement cost of the home (not the lot) is likely to be much higher than the value of the existing building. Using replacement cost on an old structure is likely to give you a value that's too high.

What is the unit price?

Sometimes investors in multifamily residential properties will simply use a unit price. For example, units might be selling for $150,000 a piece. If you have a building with 20 units, it would be worth $3 million. Unit price is further categorized by the size of the unit. For example, studios (one room with kitchen and bath—no detached bedroom) might be worth $50,000 apiece, while two-bedroom, two-bath units might go for $200,000. Again, knowing what price to ascribe to a unit comes from experience as well as from checking with agents who specialize in these properties and from other investors. Note: As with the front foot method noted above, the actual size of the unit is not taken into account. This is one of the drawbacks of this technique since, obviously, a one-bedroom unit of 800 square feet isn't going to be worth nearly as much as a one-bedroom unit of 1,200 square feet. This is another reason to use a combination of methods when evaluating property.

What is the "fixer-upper" price?

Many investors buy homes with an eye toward fixing them up and then reselling at a profit. Perhaps the fix-up will be done immediately over the course of a few weeks or months. Or, in other cases, it's done over the course of a year or more while the investors live in the home. (Living in the home while fixing it up for two years can result in significant tax savings. See Chapter 18.) It's important to understand, however, that in order to make a profit while fixing up a property, you must get a good purchase price. If you buy too high, you'll spend a lot of time and money, do a lot of work, and end up losing! To determine the fixer-upper price of a property, you must work backwards. That means that you start not with what the seller is asking, but with what you can eventually resell the property for. You should use comps and forward pricing to arrive at this figure. Then, *from the ultimate resale price* you subtract at least three things:

1. Subtract the total cost of the fix-up including a salary for yourself if you do some of the work and financing charges during the remodeling period. Be sure to get expert help in determining what the true costs will be.
2. Subtract all transaction costs involved in buying and reselling. (You might be able to reduce some of the resale costs by selling it "by owner" and not using an agent.)
3. Subtract your profit. Remember, you are operating a business and your goal is to make money.

This will let you arrive at the optimum purchase price. If you've done your homework, this purchase price should allow you to buy, do the work, and sell profitably. Be aware that the optimum purchase price is very often far below what sellers are asking, which is the reason why many savvy investors buy only 1 out of 10 or 1 out of 20 fixer-uppers that they bid on. Beware of paying too much—the overpayment will almost certainly come out of the future profits you anticipate.

What price do the leases warrant?

The value of a rental property, whether single-family, multifamily, commercial, or industrial, is affected by any leases it has on it. The leases run with the land, which essentially means that when you buy, you are normally committed to leases that the previous owner signed. When purchasing, especially commercial and industrial property, you should get a *lease abstract*, which is nothing more than a copy of, or at least the essential elements of, all leases on the property. Generally speaking, the quality of lease involves at least six elements:

1. *Length.*   Usually the longer the lease is for, assuming a good tenant, the better. On the other hand, if the lease locks you into a low rent for a long period of time, it will detract from the property's value.

2. *Tenant Quality.*   In a residential lease, this is usually determined by a credit check and by personal recommendations, including those from previous landlords. In a commercial lease, tenant quality is determined by the success of the business. A D&B (Dun and Bradstreet) report, as well as income/expense and bank statements, is often required periodically. These may be required by a lender as a condition of offering financing on a purchase.

3. *Rent Increases.*   These can be built into a lease. Sometimes they are based on the tenant's sales, as in commercial leases. There's a base rent and then a percentage of the sales on a sliding scale. Other times rent increases are tied to a cost of living index such as the CPI (Consumer Price Index). As it goes up, so too does the rent. The closer the lease is tied to actual market conditions, the better it usually is for the investor.

4. *Options.*   Many leases offer the tenant the option of renewing the lease for a period of years when it expires. If the renewal is based on a previous fixed rent, it's usually not to the investor/owner's favor. When renewal is based on an increase in rent, or at least is based on a new negotiation of rents, it is usually more favorable.

5. *Tenant Responsibilities.*   In residential leases, the tenant is usually responsible only for the general upkeep of the property (leaving it in reasonably good condition upon move-out). In commercial leases, the tenant may be responsible for maintenance, repair, upkeep, taxes, and insurance, depending on this type of lease (called *net lease,* meaning the rent is net after expenses to the owner/landlord). A *net, net, net lease* is considered optimal because the tenant covers virtually all expenses in maintaining the property.

6. *Errors.* These can be stumbling blocks, or real advantages to the investor. If the landlord/property manager is overcharging tenants (perhaps by promising back-end inducements such as reimbursements and/or refunds), then the rental income may be exaggerated, as well as the price. On the other hand, if the landlord/property manager isn't collecting all fees due (for example, not properly calculating rent based on a tenant's sales or not allocating a fee for common areas), then rents, as well as the price, may be underestimated.

A savvy investor who thoroughly investigates the leases may discover an overpriced property, or a huge bargain.

Should I get a professional appraisal?

The jury is out here. Some investors, a minority, will only move forward on the basis of a professional appraisal. Others will rely on their own or their agent's appraisal. And some simply act on their own gut feelings. It's important to remember two things about a professional appraisal. First, it can be expensive. On a single-family home, it now costs upwards of $350 to $450. On a commercial, office-building, or industrial property it can cost far more depending on the size of the building, the number of tenants, and other factors. Second, while appraisers are usually licensed, have had extensive training and experience, and belong to trade organizations that help keep them up to date on the latest techniques, what they give is still basically an opinion. It's usually an opinion based on well-accepted appraisal techniques and produced in a written report, but it's still an opinion. It's not a sale. (Usually lenders will demand a formal appraisal as a condition of offering financing.)

QUESTIONS TO ASK AN APPRAISER

What is the best method to evaluate this property?

If possible, it's a good idea to be present at the appraisal. For one thing, it assures you that an actual appraisal was done. In the recent past, some appraisers of residential real estate, for example, often just did a "drive-by." Here they would simply drive by the street and stop in front of the house, sometimes taking a picture of it, without even getting out of their cars. Then, they would write up the appraisal based on comps and the outside appearance of the house. Obviously, this is not what most buyers are paying for. A thorough appraisal will involve a physical inspection of the property. And in the case of commercial or industrial property, it may include an evaluation of tenants and leases. If you meet the inspector, you can ask what the best method of appraisal for the subject property happens to be. For most residential property, it will simply be a matter of assessing comps. However, it could involve a replacement cost technique or even the use of a multiplier. While this question may or may not be answered in the written report, it will certainly be answered if you ask the question directly of an appraiser.

What is the quality of the comps?

Where an appraiser is relying almost entirely on comps, as may be the case in residential property, you should inquire as to whether there truly are good comps available. As noted in earlier questions, if the property is located in a large tract of similar homes, it's likely that many comps will be obtainable. On the other hand, if it's a custom home, finding truly similar comps could be a problem. If there aren't good comps readily available, you should be sure to ask the appraiser where he or she is getting market price figures from. It could be from homes some distance away that are not truly similar to yours. You may even want to suggest areas that you feel are similar for the appraiser to use. Don't expect the appraiser always to react with appreciation to your suggestions, however. Most appraisers are wary of owners as well as buyers who want to influence the outcome of the appraisal. Nevertheless, if you have a valid point to make with regard to comps, be sure to be assertive enough to get the appraiser to listen. Most have an open mind and will listen.

Will you physically examine the property yourself?

The appraiser, the one who's licensed and whom you are paying, is supposed to get out there and take a look at the property. Unfortunately, this is not always the case. When there is an especially heavy demand for appraisals, as was the case during the first few years of the century when falling interest rates and resulting refinances created a huge demand, some appraisers sent out "assistants" who might have been their kids, or some hired person who wasn't thoroughly qualified. That's another reason to meet the appraiser at the property. (You can always say you need to meet the appraiser there because you have the key to let him/her in.) Another concern is that the appraiser actually goes through the property. This usually means examining it from the exterior, including taking measurements of the lot and building. It also means going inside and looking around. Note: Appraisers often see dozens of buildings in a single day. They may be able to absorb in a glance what it would take you half an hour to analyze. Don't be surprised if the appraiser is in and out of a typical house in 15 minutes or less, unless there's some sort of problem. Also, remember that an appraiser isn't going to assess the systems of the house (plumbing, electrical, heating/air, and so forth) that's the job of a professional inspector.

8

Have You Calculated Transaction Costs?

QUESTIONS TO ASK YOURSELF

Do I understand transaction costs?

No matter what you buy or sell, there are usually transaction costs (also called *closing costs*.) When you buy/sell stock, you pay a broker's fee. When you buy/sell a car there are licensing fees, taxes, and other charges. Real estate is no different, except that the transaction costs involved are often much higher than for most other items. (An exception could be a rarity such as a painting, where auction houses sometimes charge the buyers *and* the sellers each as much as 20 percent of the sales figure!) As an investor, it behooves you to use a sharp pencil to determine just what those costs may be, and, if possible, to find ways to reduce them. Remember, the price does *not* normally include the transaction costs. They are added on. In most real estate transactions, a round trip (costs for both buying and later reselling a property) averages about 10 percent. That means on a $250,000 property, the costs could be $25,000, and on a million dollar property, they could be $100,000. It may very well be the case that a property that seems like a good investment based just on the purchase price could turn into a loser once the transaction costs are added in.

What are the transaction costs when purchasing?

Transaction costs can be estimated. However, they will vary with each transaction. Most, though not all, are based on the price of the property. When purchasing a property, most of the transaction costs usually involve the financing, though there are other costs as well. Here are some of the costs you can expect to pay when making a purchase:

1. *Points.*   Most lenders charge points (one point equals 1 percent of the loan amount). On a residential property, it's not unusual to pay anywhere from one to five points, depending on a variety of factors. These factors include market condition, your credit rating, the quality of the property, and so on.

2. *Loan Fees.*   These are additional charges the lender may impose as a condition of getting the financing. In recent years, these have *all* been labeled, "garbage fees." Actually, some lender's fees—the true charges for securing the loan that the lender is passing on to the borrower—may be perfectly legitimate. For example, the lender may pass on a $350 fee for an appraisal or a $35 fee for a credit report, and this is not usually considered unreasonable. On the other hand, other fees such as lender's attorney, drawing documents, loan administration, and so on, which should either be a normal cost of doing business to a lender, or which are marked up, are usually considered unreasonable by most investors.

3. *Buyer's Agent's Commission*   Some buyers use an agent other than the seller's agent to find a property. While buyer's agents usually are able to get their fee paid out of the seller's agent's commission, that's not always the case. Sometimes there will be a separate buyer's agent's commission, typically 3 percent on a residential property, 5 to 10 percent on bare land.

4. *Title Insurance and Escrow.*   These are typically split between buyer and seller, although in some locales the buyer pays all of one and the seller all of the other, and in other locales, buyer or seller pay all of the fees.

5. *Broker's Transaction Fee.*   This is usually considered a "garbage fee." It is added on by the realty company, not the agent you're dealing with. In residential properties it has been running from $350 to $650. It compensates the agency for its costs in doing business.

6. *Buyer's Attorney and Other Incidental Costs.*   If you use an attorney, you'll have this fee. Incidental costs

can be anything from having documents sent to you by an express service to having them copied and notarized.

What are the transaction costs when selling?

The seller's transaction costs are similar to the buyer's with two significant differences. First, there are usually no loan fees, unless a lender charges something such as a prepayment penalty for paying off the mortgage early. Second, unless the seller sells entirely "by owner," there's a commission. Here are some of the costs you can expect to pay when reselling an investment property:

1. *Seller's Agent's Commission.*   The commission is usually based on the value of the property and is completely negotiable. Most agents ask 6 percent for full-service selling of a home, 10 percent for bare land, and anywhere from 5 to 10 percent for commercial/industrial property. Industry sources indicate that the actual full-service commission paid on residential property is closer to 4½ to 5 percent nationwide. If you sell the property "by owner," you may nevertheless want to pay a buyer's agent a commission for finding a buyer for you. This typically amounts to half a full-service commission, so if that is 6 percent, this would amount to 3 percent. Discount brokers are available nationwide and most offer full-service commissions at 4 to 5 percent. There are also some fee-for-service agents who charge a set amount per service offered. For example, it might cost $500 for them to provide a purchase agreement.

2. *Title Insurance and Escrow.*   These are typically split between buyer and seller, although in some locales the buyer pays all of one and the seller all of the other, and in other locales, buyer or seller pays all of the fees.

3. *Broker's Transaction Fee.*   This is usually considered a "garbage fee." It is added on by the realty company, not the agent you're dealing with. In residential properties it has been running from $350 to $650. It compensates the agency for its costs in doing business.

4. *Seller's Attorney and Other Incidental Costs.*   If you use an attorney, you'll have this fee. Incidental costs can

be anything from having documents sent to you by express service to having them copied and notarized.

Can I get the sellers to pay some of my costs?

One way of reducing your transaction costs is to get the other party to pay for them. If you're a buyer, that means asking the seller to do it. If you're getting financing, as most investors are, that means asking the seller to pay for your *nonrecurring costs*. These include such things as title insurance, escrow fees, and perhaps some points. *Recurring charges* are such things as your mortgage payment, insurance, and tax payments. Most lenders will not fund a transaction where buyer's *recurring* closing costs are being paid by the seller. They will when the seller pays the *nonrecurring* costs. Sellers, of course, are most certainly not going to be happy about paying any of your costs. Hence, in order to get them to comply, you must make it a condition of the sale. "I'll buy your property *if* you pay some or all of my recurring costs." It's actually inserted in the purchase agreement as a contingency. In a strong market or in a situation where you're low-balling the price, sellers are most likely to tell you to take a hike. They figure another buyer will soon come by. But, when the market's slow and buyers are few and far between, they may agree. Note that offering a better price is an inducement to a seller to compromise and agree to pay some of your closing costs. It's something to consider if you're cash poor.

Will the buyer pay some of my costs?

When it's time to resell, the shoe is on the other foot. Now you're the seller of the property and you have some hefty transaction costs to pay, the largest of which is normally the commission. Can you get the buyer to pay these costs for you? (Note: If you can transfer the transaction costs for the roundtrip—buying and selling—to the other party, you may save as much as 10 percent of the cost of the acquisition!) Again, a lot depends on price and market conditions. In a hot seller's market, as was the case in the early to mid-2000s, sellers frequently could demand both a high price and that buyers pay some or all of their closing costs. (Since there's seldom lender concern for a seller, all of the costs are up for grabs.) As the market cools, however, it becomes more of a case of trading price for closing costs. In most markets you can't expect to get both a high price for the property and sellers who will pay the closing costs.

Will the agent cut the commission?

Another way to reduce your costs when you resell your investment property is to negotiate a lower commission. This can be done at two separate times. The first is when you list with an agent. (The second is discussed in the question below.) Most full-service (meaning they do everything for you as part of their service) agents will begin by asking for a 6 percent commission. In some parts of the country, they will stick with that. However, in other parts, particularly the Northwest, they will sometimes negotiate a lower commission rate. Nationally, the rate of commission is reported to be around 5 percent or less, and falling. Of course, if you want to perform some of the agent's functions (such as showing the home yourself or paying for some advertisements), most areas have discount brokers. They will list the property for as little as 4 percent. (Remember, 3 percent *usually* goes to the buyer's broker, so the seller's (your) broker is only getting 1 percent.) If you're interested in a discount broker try www.helpUsell.com or www.assist2sell.com. Finally, you can attempt to sell your property "by owner." (Try www.owners.com for more info.) If you're successful, you will have saved the entire cost of the commission. Many by-owner sellers, however, are willing to pay half a commission, typically 3 percent, to a broker who brings in a buyer ready, willing, and able to make the purchase. It's a case of getting a quick sale or waiting it out. Keep in mind, however, that most buyers' brokers will not help you with your end of the transaction. Rather, that's going to be up to you.

Can I insist that the agent cut the commission?

My suggestion is that besides simply asking, you never lean on an agent who is listing your property to reduce the commission rate he or she wants. The reason is that in order to get a sale for a good price, you need that agent's full cooperation and enthusiasm. An agent who finally agrees to take a listing for less than he or she feels they are worth may simply not work hard for you. It's better to simply say no to this agent and find another who will work hard for less. On the other hand, once you've signed a listing commission and a buyer is in hand, you can pressure the agent to lower the commission. This is usually done when the agent presents an offer for less than the asking price. (If it's a full price offer, you may owe a commission even if you don't sell.) For example, you're asking $400,000 and the agent brings in an offer for $350,000. The buyers won't go a penny higher. So you tell the agent that in order to make the deal, he or she will have to contribute, that is, cut their commission. Agents hate to be put in this situation. They feel they've done their job when they bring in a buyer. But, if it's not for full price, then they actually haven't. To make the deal, some agents will, in fact, cut the price. Others will refuse. A lot depends on how good a negotiator you are and how hard you stick to your guns. Just don't fight so hard that you end up losing a sale that you really need!

Will the lender reduce its costs?

Sometimes lenders will. Most investors, when buying, don't think you can negotiate with a lender, and in a super-heated market, such as we've recently had, that was true. If you didn't take the deal—including costs—that the lender was offering, there were 20 people in line behind you who would. However, as the market has slowed, lenders have become more flexible. While few will actually deal on the interest rate (which is often a fixed cost to them), they may reduce some of their fees or even provide you with a no-fee mortgage. It's important to remember, however, that the time to negotiate with a lender is when you first apply for the mortgage. At that time, if the lender isn't agreeable, you can easily walk away and find another lender—there's no shortage of them. On the other hand, if you wait until you've found a property and are ready to close the deal, you have no leverage. If you don't take the loan that's offered, it could take you weeks to apply for and get approved by another lender. And in the interim, you could lose the deal.

Will the lender finance some costs?

Lenders are increasingly willing to do this. There are two approaches. One is by rolling the closing costs into the mortgage, thus ending up with a higher loan. The other is by increasing the interest rate slightly, but maintaining the same mortgage amount. The first method usually involves the price paid for the property. For example, when buying, instead of offering the seller $300,000, you offer $310,000, with the seller paying $10,000 of your closing costs and a zero down mortgage. This is essentially the same offer to the seller. Either way, he or she nets out $300,000. However, at the higher price, all financed by the mortgage, you get $10,000 to use toward your closing costs. Assuming that the property appraises for the higher figure, there should be no problem. However, some lenders will refuse to fund such loans if they see the price has been increased as part of a counteroffer on the purchase agreement. Therefore, it's important to work this out with the seller in advance of completing a purchase agreement. Another method is simply to ask the lender to pay all of your nonrecurring closing costs. In exchange, you will agree to a slightly higher interest rate (usually about three-eighths of 1 percent) and a correspondingly slightly higher monthly payment. Today, probably the majority of lenders will work with you on this. However, if your lender won't, seek out another that is more cooperative.

Can I save on costs by getting a real estate license?

Some investors do, and there can be some advantages. For example, as an agent and a Realtor® (member of the National Association of Realtors) you can sign up with your local real estate board and get the multiple listings, for a hefty fee. This can be a terrific help when you're scouting for properties, particularly if you can get them as they first come out. On the other hand, just about any real estate agent can give you at least limited access (and sometimes full access) to these same listings. Further, virtually all properties today are listed on the Internet somewhere, for instance the Web site www.realtor.com. In addition, as an agent you can demand a portion of the commission when you buy property. You can represent yourself and, at least in theory, get the buyer's agent's half (usually around 3 percent) of the purchase price. That can be a substantial amount of money. The downside is that unless you want to actually become an agent and sell property to others for a living, getting a license will cost you time and money, and joining a real estate board, as noted above, can also be expensive. Further, having a license normally means you will need to disclose that fact to sellers when you're a buyer. Failure to disclose could result in a seller's coming back at you after the sale and saying that because you were a broker, you had an unfair advantage in the transaction. It could cost you the deal as well as damages. And disclosing you're an agent can put some sellers off. It can certainly put off some lenders, many of whom don't like to make their best loans to real estate agents. They suspect that the agents may be making creative deals and they worry that what's stated on the purchase agreement, which is their guiding document, may not reflect the true deal. This is particularly the case when there's a commission going to the buyer of the home who also happens to be an agent. In short, agents sometimes get lousier financing. My suggestion is that if you're going to invest, just be an investor. Usually you don't need an agent's license. (Although, as noted, getting the agent's knowledge is very worthwhile.)

Will the title company cut its costs?

Sometimes. If the property you're purchasing was previously sold within the last three years or so, it makes the title search easier. You can ask for a "reissue rate." The reduction can be as much as one-third off the regular price. As far as getting the title company to negotiate a lower price, it really depends on the state you're living in (in some states title insurance costs are regulated) and how good a customer you are. If you're bringing in three or four deals a year to the title company, chances are it will be happy to cut you a better price. On the other hand, if this is a one-timer, chances are the title company won't pay much attention to your request. Keep in mind that the party who pays the title insurance costs (including title abstract and title search) is fully negotiable. You can demand that the seller pay for these items. As noted above, if the seller is anxious to sell in a weak market and likes your price, you could get these costs transferred.

Will the escrow company cut its costs?

□

Again, it depends. You usually can't get a reissue reduced fee because the running of the escrow is roughly the same amount of work regardless of how many times the property is sold. Of course, as noted above, a lot depends on how good a customer you are. If you're bringing in several deals a year, chances are the escrow company will be happy to cut you a better price. On the other hand, if this is a one-timer, chances are the escrow company won't pay much attention to your demands. Keep in mind that the party who pays the escrow costs, just as who pays the title insurance costs, is usually negotiable. You can demand that the seller pay for these items. As noted above, if the seller is anxious to sell in a weak market and likes your price, you could get these costs transferred. Also keep in mind that in recent years some unscrupulous escrow companies have jacked up their fees to the point where they are way out of line in terms of what competitors charge and what the market will bear. Be sure to check out the fee structure of the escrow company you are planning to use before opening escrow so that you won't get overcharged.

QUESTIONS TO ASK OTHERS

Is the commission rate negotiable?

□

You'll want to ask your agent this when you're selling and sometimes even when you're buying (using a buyer's agent that you have to pay). The answer is that it certainly is negotiable—there is no set rate anywhere in the country. Having said that, keep in mind that some agents have a minimum commission rate they charge, and they won't work for anything less. As noted earlier, if the agent says he or she wants a specific rate and won't budge, it's probably a better idea to simply look for a different agent. Pressuring someone to work for less than they think acceptable is the surest way to get poor service.

How much are the closing costs?

□

A good agent should be able to come within a hundred bucks of telling you what your closing costs will be.

Sometimes agents will want you to use a particular title/escrow company. Many agents insist that both buyers and sellers use an escrow and title insurance affiliated with their real estate company. They often say that this is a title/escrow company they've used in the past and that they feel comfortable it will handle everything correctly and at minimum costs. Just remember, however, that it's up to you (and the other party) to decide on which escrow and title insurance company to use. The agent can suggest, but cannot normally demand. Note that the bundling of services (where the agent gets a kickback) is unethical and, in some cases, illegal, but recommending an affiliated company usually isn't, so long as the affiliation is disclosed and you agree to it. Also keep in mind that if you're the seller, RESPA (the Real Estate Settlement Procedure Act) says that you cannot dictate what title insurance company a buyer may use.

How much will title insurance cost?

Be sure that you ask this of the title insurance company *before* you hire it. While, as noted earlier, some states fix the rates with a sliding scale based on the sales price, others allow negotiations. Try to find out if the home was recently sold. If it was sold within the previous few years, ask for a reissue rate. It can save you a considerable amount of money if the title company is willing. When you discuss price with the title company, be sure you know with whom you're dealing. If it's simply the clerk in the front who answers the phone, chances are the answer is going to be, "Sorry." On the other hand, if you deal with one of the officers of the company, then you have a chance of striking a bargain. Never be afraid to point out how many deals you're bringing the title insurance company. The more deals, the better client you are. And many companies have a special discount rate for their best clients.

How much will the escrow fee be?

Sometimes, but not always, the escrow company will be associated with the title company. Either way, be sure to get a written estimate of the costs you're likely to incur for the escrow portion of the service. Keep in mind that a firm figure can be elusive since it can be hard to nail costs down to the penny in advance. However, barring something unusual, an escrow officer should be able to tell you, in writing, what the costs will be to within a hundred dollars or so. Be sure to check if the escrow company charges a single overall fee, or whether it itemizes. If it's the overall fee, be sure that, in fact, everything is covered and that there aren't additional charges that could crop up later on. If it's itemized, try to get a total figure for all of the itemized costs.

Can I reduce the points for a higher interest rate?

Most investors are strapped for cash. Thus, when a lender tells you that, yes, the mortgage you want is available on your $600,000 purchase, but it will cost you three points, you're likely to cringe. That's an added $18,000 in cash you'll need to come up with. An alternative is to ask the lender to substitute points for a slightly higher interest rate. Today, many lenders will go along. The actual substitution ratio will vary depending on the lender and market conditions, but it usually works out to be ⅛ to ⅜ of a percent increase in the mortgage interest rate for each point taken off. For example, if you're borrowing $100,000 at 6 percent and three points and the substitution rate is ⅛ of a percent, your new interest rate for a no points mortgage would be 6⅜ percent. Keep in mind that this, of course, will be reflected in a somewhat higher payment. It goes the other way around as well. If you're cash rich and want to cut your payment, you can offer to pay points for a reduced interest rate. On the above mortgage, you might pay six points and get the interest rate reduced to 5 ¼ percent, with a reduced monthly payment as well.

Can I roll the closing costs into the financing?

It can be easier to do than you may realize. Just ask the lender. On residences, some Fannie Mae and Freddie Mac underwritten programs offer automatic closing cost inclusion. (Fannie Mae and Freddie Mac are the big secondary lenders who "buy" mortgages from the banks and other lenders with whom you directly deal.) Their loans may be increased in amount, sometimes to over 103 percent of the property's value to accommodate the buyer's closing costs. In other cases, the lender may have a program already in place where it will be happy to pay your closing costs for you, so long as you're willing to pay a slightly higher interest rate.

Can I get a reappraisal?

Nothing will put a pall on a deal faster than to have an appraiser come in and tell you that the property isn't worth what you're offering to pay for it. Remember, the appraisal normally occurs *after* the purchase agreement has been signed. Without an appraisal for the full purchase price, it may be impossible for you to make the deal because you won't be able to get the right financing. Don't think that you paid too much just because the appraisal's low. It could be a bad appraisal. Ask the lender for a reappraisal. Keep in mind, however, that this could cost you an additional appraisal fee. And the lender could send out the same appraiser with the same result. It might be better to seek out a different lender.

Can we renegotiate the price?

When the house doesn't appraise out, it could indeed mean that it is overpriced. You may want to sit down with the seller and show him or her the appraisal. Sometimes, faced with such evidence, a seller will agree to the lower appraised price. Thus, a bad appraisal might actually be good for you, the investor!

9

Where Do You Find Good Investment Homes and Properties?

QUESTIONS TO ASK YOURSELF

Have I checked the Internet?

Today, better than 90 percent of all properties for sale are listed somewhere on the Internet. Most agent-listed properties can be located on sites such as www.realtor.com. Many FSBO (for sale by owner) properties are listed on the independent sites such as www.owners.com or www.fsbo.com. Other sites including www.yahoo.com and even www.msn.com can link you to sites that offer properties for sale. Thus, as an investor, you really do need to have a good computer and a high-speed access channel to the Internet. Some of your best hunting can be done in the comfort of your home working at the keyboard. Be careful, however, to pay special attention to the *location* of properties. The Internet is international in scope and it's just as easy to pull up a listing in Manhattan as in Madrid. Also, don't become so enamored with Internet listings that you fail to recognize the basics of property investing—you need to physically check them out. Go there, walk through, look at the neighborhood, and do it many times before you buy. Don't be tempted to make a purchase based on written descriptions and images found on a Web site.

Have I contacted an agent about local listings?

It's important to work with a local agent(s) in order to find properties that are listed for sale in your immediate area. Agents "farm" nearby neighborhoods for listings. Sometimes they'll get a listing and "vest pocket" it for a few days before reporting it to the MLS (Multiple Listing Service)—and then it could take days before it gets to other brokers, and possibly even weeks before it gets onto the Internet sites. Vest pocketing a listing simply means holding onto it so that other agents can't work on it. It's strictly forbidden by most real estate cooperatives, such as the MLS. However, it nonetheless sometimes still gets done. The agent hopes to find a buyer so that he or she won't have to split a commission. If you're working with that agent, you could be that buyer. Further, agents sometimes know well in advance when a house is likely to come onto the market. They could be working with the seller for months, coaching him or her on how to prepare the property, determine the right price, when to time the sale, and so on. Thus, the agent can get you set up to make a purchase as soon as the property is listed, long before other competing investors find out. Finally, an agent can help you with listed property. An agent's expertise can give you advice on when a seller might be willing to accept a lower offer or is ready to cut the price. The agent can provide valuable information on values, neighborhoods, and more. An investor who doesn't work with an agent(s) has one hand tied behind his or her back.

Have I worked the "stale" listings?

"Stale" refers to listings of homes that haven't sold for a long time. A seller who puts a property on the market on Monday isn't likely to cut the price by Friday. On the other hand, a seller who's had his or her property on the market for three months with no activity is likely to be very anxious to make a deal . . . and cut the price to do it. In other words, look for the "stale" listings, those which have been out there the longest. Keep in mind that a typical listing is for 90 days. As you get closer to the end of that time, the agent is more likely to put pressure on the seller to accept any offer. After all, unless the seller decides to renew, usually after 90 days, the agent has lost the listing—and a commission. In a normal market, a large number of properties will be in the stale category. Indeed, most properties will take two months or more to sell. In a slow market, you'll want to extend your timeframe to homes that have gone unsold for six months or longer. In a hot market, however, you will have to reduce that time frame . . . sometimes to a few weeks.

Have I looked for price reductions?

When a seller cuts the price on a property, it's an indication that he or she is anxious to sell. The seller is sending out an appeal to buyers. "Look at my property and *please* make an offer!" But, pay particular attention to the amount of the price reduction. A seller who cuts the price by a thousand dollars is merely trying to attract attention. A seller who cuts the price by $10,000 is seriously eager to sell. Very anxious sellers will make repeated price reductions, sometimes every week. That's a seller to pay attention to. Keep in mind that when you find a property that has been reduced in price and which otherwise seems suitable, don't feel obligated to offer the current asking price. Just because a seller has reduced the price doesn't mean it's at rock bottom. Treat a reduced price as you would any other—the starting point for negotiations. Work down from there. In addition, check the wording that comes with the price reduction. It's often a clue as to how eager the seller is to dump the property. Look for such phrases as, "Highly motivated" or "Bring in all offers," or "Wants to move immediately." You get the idea. The agent is sending out the word that this seller is very anxious and will even consider low-ball offers. If this is combined with price reductions, you probably have a real opportunity in the making.

Have I done "drive throughs"?

One of the best ways to find properties is simply to drive through the neighborhoods in which you're interested. You can think of this as your "farm." You'll define certain neighborhoods and on a fairly regular basis drive or walk them. Look for signs that indicate a person is getting ready to sell a home, such as painting and fixing it up. When you find a home that looks suitable, stop by and engage the seller/owner in discussion. Find out what the asking price is and any special features. Then check it out: do a CMA (comparative market analysis). Remember, if the owner is getting ready to sell, he or she will be very happy to talk with you. You promise the opportunity to save that seller a commission, or at least part of one. If you come up with a reasonable offer, the seller may go ahead and let you purchase the property directly, even before it gets on the market. Chances are you'll have found a real bargain. A word of warning, however: don't be like "the blind leading the blind." If neither you nor the seller has any serious experience in real estate, pay an attorney or a good agent to handle the transaction for you. (You needn't pay a big commission. Many attorneys and agents will handle the paperwork for a reasonable fee.) You want to be sure that you get clear title and that you don't open yourself to an angry seller's later coming back at you for some error in the transaction.

Have I considered buying a foreclosure?

Most people believe that if you can pick up a property in foreclosure, it's automatically a good deal. That's not necessarily the case. Some are . . . and some aren't. A good number of investors, however, make a handsome living by buying up and then renting out and/or reselling foreclosures. If this appeals to you, check into Chapter 15.

Have I looked at REOs?

REO stands for "real estate owned" and it refers to property that a lender has taken back through foreclosure. Lenders hate this kind of property because on their books it shows up as a liability instead of as an asset. Therefore, they are very anxious to get rid of REOs. However, not so anxious that they're willing to take a loss if there's any way to avert it. The big plus for you in dealing with a lender over dealing with a home seller in foreclosure is that it's a cleaner deal. There's no crying or recriminations. Also, you can usually get title insurance and sometimes the bank often will even help you with the financing! The downside is that lenders don't like to admit publicly that they have a REO problem. Many won't admit they even have any REOs. Thus, you can't usually just walk in and ask to buy one. (REOs show up as liabilities on the books of lenders. Too many REOs lead to insolvency.) On the other hand, the lender wants to get out from under the REO by selling it, therefore it needs you.

How do I find REOs?

While lenders often keep quiet about REOs as far as the general public is concerned, they are often open about them to legitimate investors. (They also often list them for everyone to see with an agent, but at that point they typically want top dollar.) To find hidden REOs, you need to let the lender know that you understand what a REO is and that you'd like to bid on one. Once the lender understands that you're special, and not part of the public that is only interested in deposits and checking accounts, it might open up. When checking with a lender, look for the person in charge. The first step is to ask for the "operations officer," who handles day-to-day operations. Then ask to see the officer who deals in REOs. Then you need to make a case that you're an investor who has the means and desire to purchase. For more information on REOs, check into Chapter 15.

Have I looked at HUD repos?

Since most mortgages are insured, guaranteed, or funded by the federal government, the number of homes the government has taken back is enormous. Of course, it doesn't want this property, so it's always trying to sell it. You can sometimes take advantage of these sales to get into a property at a bargain price. The Housing and Urban Development Department (HUD) takes back homes mainly through its FHA (Federal Housing Administration) program. The FHA insures lenders who make loans. When a borrower defaults, the FHA makes good the loan to the lender and takes the property back. At any given time, it may have tens of thousands of repossessed homes (repos) for sale across the country. Most HUD properties are going to be single-family homes in the moderate to low price range, although multifamily dwellings do show up. Additionally, they may not be in the best of condition. You can check to see if there are any HUD homes in your area on the Internet at www.hud.gov/homes/index.cfm.

How do I make HUD an offer?

To make an offer, you must work through an agent who represents HUD in your local area. (HUD can refer you to these.) HUD tries to sell its homes at fair market price. Occasionally, particularly if you are sharp at knowing property values, you can find some real bargains here. HUD doesn't make loans directly, but it does work with lenders in a variety of programs. You may be able to get in with virtually nothing down, so long as you're intending to occupy the home. If you're buying as an investment, HUD will usually want at least 10 percent down. As with many government programs, HUD aims to sell its homes to those who will occupy them. Read this as *not* to investors. Thus, in the initial "offer period" those who intend to occupy the HUD homes are given priority in their offers. If you're looking for both a house to live in *and* an investment, this can be the perfect choice for you.

Can I invest/buy from HUD?

Most HUD homes are not in great shape and most owner/occupants are not eager to buy into them. Further, HUD makes an effort to offer them at market price. Thus, for casual home owner/occupant buyers who don't really know the market, it may not seem like there are any bargains here. As a result, very often these homes are sold to investors. If there are no owner/occupants who submit offers during the initial offer period, or the home does not sell in that time frame, then investors can make offers that will be considered. In addition, if the home is in bad shape, HUD may offer a fix-up allowance. HUD may also offer special incentives if it's particularly interested in moving a property. For owner/occupants, this can include a moving allowance. For investors, this can include a bonus (price reduction) for closing the sale fast. If you have all your financing ducks in a row and can close within a week or two, it can mean a significant financial difference. Of course, you'll want to have a professional inspection of the home. However, unlike conventional purchases where the professional inspection is normally conducted *after* you've signed a purchase agreement with the seller, with HUD you'll need to make your inspection *beforehand*. HUD doesn't like to tie up homes on contingencies that involve inspections.

Have I looked at VA repos?

Unlike HUD, which *insures* loans to lenders, the VA (Department of Veterans Affairs) *guarantees* the performance of a loan to a lender. If the borrower defaults, the VA pays off its guaranteed portion. However, rather than simply pay out cash, the VA buys the property from the lender who forecloses and then resells it. Initially only veterans who qualify (were on active duty during specific time periods) can get VA loans in order to buy a home. After the VA has foreclosed, however, it opens the homes to anyone who wants to buy them, veteran or nonveteran, investor or owner/occupant.

How do I, as an investor, purchase a VA repo?

To purchase a VA home, as with the HUD program, you must go through a local real estate agent who represents the VA's property management program. Typically these agents will advertise in local newspapers. You may also find most, but not all, of them listed on the VA's property management Web site, www.homeloans.va.gov/homes.html. In order to make an actual offer, you must go through an agent and use the proper forms. These include the following: Offer to Purchase/Contract of Sale (VA form 26-6705) and Credit Statement (VA form 26-6705B). The VA will handle financing. However, it prefers to do this for owner/occupants. And it gives priority to buyers who come in with their own financing (cash to the VA). You'll usually, though not always, do better if you handle your own financing outside the VA.

Am I ready to fix up a VA repo?

As with HUD homes, many of the VA properties are in the same condition as when they were turned over after foreclosure. In the past, however, the VA has had an extensive program of refurbishing properties in order to get a higher market value. If you buy a refurbished home, don't expect to get any kind of bargain on the price. How the homes are handled is largely determined by the regional VA property management office. Again, you'll want to have a professional inspection so that you'll know what you're getting. However, as with HUD, you'll need to conduct the inspection during the offering period and not after you have your offer accepted. The agent who's handling the house can arrange for you and your inspector to get in. Be sure you use a sharp pencil when you calculate how much the property is really worth.

Have I checked out Fannie Mae properties?

Fannie Mae along with Freddie Mac, which is discussed next, are the main secondary residential lenders in the country. If a borrower fails to make a mortgage payment and falls into foreclosure, it's often Fannie Mae or Freddie Mac (through whatever lender happens to be servicing the mortgage at the time) that takes the property back. Those agencies then have to get rid of it. This, again, can present an opportunity for investors. Fannie Mae underwrites all types of single-family homes, which include detached properties, condos, and townhomes. Most of their inventory consists of fairly new homes, and often they are in modest to even up-scale neighborhoods. Fannie Mae also requires you to go through a local real estate agent. However, the agents are required to list all the homes on the local MLS, so there's no difficulty in gaining access. You can also find a list of Fannie Mae homes at its Web site: www.fanniemae.com/homes.html.

How do I handle a Fannie Mae purchase?

The transaction is handled just as if you were dealing with any other conventional seller. Unlike dealing with either HUD or the VA, you can add contingencies and other conditions with your offer. You may demand to have a professional home inspection *after* the offer is accepted. You can also negotiate over terms, down payment, and financing. Fannie Mae will not, however, accept a contingency that first requires the sale of an existing home. You may use your own title insurance and escrow company. However, usually in order to have your offer accepted, you must be preapproved by a lender. That means that you've had your credit checked or had income and cash on deposit verified. These are repos, which means they may (or may not) be in poor condition. Sometimes Fannie Mae will fix up these properties in order to get a higher price. Sometimes they are left in the condition they were received. In any event, the homes are all sold in "as is" condition, meaning the buyer must take them with whatever problems they have at the time of sale. Fannie Mae does offer its own REO financing. However, it's typically not any better than you get elsewhere.

Have I checked out Freddie Mac properties?

Freddie Mac offers single-family detached houses, condos, and townhomes. However, Freddie Mac generally cleans and fixes up its homes before offering them for sale. If you want to submit an offer on a home and do the fix-up work yourself, chances are that Freddie Mac will, at the least, clean up the property before you buy it. Through its HomeSteps program, Freddie Mac will offer homes to owner/occupants at competitive interest rates with low down payments of 5 percent and no mortgage insurance. It will also offset some of the title and escrow costs. These homes, however, are almost all competitively priced at market. Freddie Mac homes are offered through a select group of lenders. To find out more about them, check into www.homesteps.com.

Have I checked out other government programs?

Many other government programs offer repos. Sometimes there are only a few properties for sale. At other times there may be hundreds. Further, in some of the programs you can find commercial, multi-unit residential, office, and industrial properties. Following is a list of government Web sites you may find helpful. For more information on finding investment properties, you should check out my book *How to Find Hidden Real Estate Bargains*, Second Edition, McGraw-Hill, 2003. This list and portions of this material also appear in my book *How to Get Started in Real Estate Investing*, McGraw-Hill, 2003.

Customs
   www.treas.gov/auction.customs
Department of Veteran Affairs
   www.homeloans.va.gov/homes.htm

Federal Deposit Insurance Corporation
www.fdic.gov/buying/owner/index.html

GSA
http://propertydisposal.gsa.gov/property/propforsale/

IRS
www.treas.gov/auctions/irs/real/html

Small Business Administration
http://appl.sba.gov/pfsales/dsp_search.html

U.S. Marshals Service
www.usdoj.gov/marshals/assets/nsl.htm

U.S. Army Corps of Engineers
www.sas.usace.armyu.mil/hapinv/haphomes.htm

10

Do You Have
a Good Agent?

QUESTIONS TO ASK YOURSELF

How do I find an "investor's agent"?

Every investor has to ask this question. There are over a million agents in the country. But probably more than 95 percent of them cater mainly to people who are looking for a home in which to live. Yes, if you ask about a single-family home as an investment, they'll show them to you. But they may not know the difference between a home that will make a good residence in which to live and one that will make a good investment. (See the previous chapters if you're still not sure.) The agent you want should be handling investment properties as his or her primary line of work. Residences for occupant/owners should only be a sideline. Don't hesitate to ask your agent the *type* of properties he or she has sold over the last year. If the answer is single-family homes, then ask if the buyers have all moved in. If they have, then chances are you've got the wrong agent. You want one who will tell you that he or she has sold strip malls, apartment buildings, office buildings, bare land, investment homes, and more. This is an agent who can lead you to good investment properties and get the right kind of deal for you.

Is my agent experienced?

You want not only an agent who is trustworthy in the sense of looking out for your interests and straightforward and honest, you also want an agent whose experience you can trust. This means someone who's been in the business a while and seen it through many deals, who can truly advise you not just on buying a home, but on investing. While the majority of agents come into the business for a few years to try their hands, only a relative few stick it out for decades and make a career of selling real estate. Nevertheless, every town does have some of these career real estate people. Traditionally, such an experienced agent would be a one-person office. You could simply ask other agents who has been around the longest, or call the local real estate board and see if they will tell you which brokerage has the greatest longevity. However, in today's modern world, most successful real estate people have gone under the umbrella of a national or franchise company such as Coldwell-Banker, Century 21, ReMAX, Prudential, or some other. However, even in one of these offices, there is often an agent who specializes in investment property. That's the person to look for. You want someone who's been around for a minimum of 5 years and preferably for 20 years.

How do I avoid the wrong agent?

You're looking for an agent who will take the time to work with you to find just the right property. My experience is that too many "hot" agents just churn and burn. They hop from prospect to prospect, and if you don't buy within the first showing or two, they'll dump you and move on. After all, they have a certain volume of sales to maintain. That's probably fortunate, because if you stuck with this person, you might end up with a property you wouldn't want. As an investor, you don't want to be the victim of someone who processes real estate buyers in a quick and dirty fashion and whose eye is riveted to his or her bottom line. Rather, what you want is someone who is successful enough to have the time to invest in his or her clients, who is willing to take as much time as necessary to service them, who is determined to get for them just what they want.

What does the "right" agent's profile look like?

Actually, you're looking for someone who's been in the business long enough to become financially secure— someone who doesn't really need you! These persons should, ideally, own investment properties on their own, so that they know what it is to invest and to be landlords. Further, they should have enough income from their own investments that they don't need to churn and burn, to turn over prospects quickly in order to maintain a high volume and a high income just from sales. The right agent will, of course, be trustworthy, straightforward, and honest. In addition, he or she probably has the following profile:

Assertive, but Not Pushy.   The ideal agent must be assertive enough to tell you when you're wrong and to deal effectively in negotiations with the other party. Beware of agents who are too aggressive. While you may think that you'll be turning them loose on the other party, you may find they are actually applying enormous pressure on you to act quickly, and not necessarily on what you really want.

Been in Business for Several Years.   Remember, it takes a while to build up a string of properties and accumulate wealth in real estate. It's not usually done overnight. That's not to say a young agent can't be terrific. It's just that time usually is the best teacher.

Successful.   It's possible to be in real estate and never really make it. There are a lot of agents who are at the periphery of the field. Typically these have outside incomes, perhaps retirement from another field. They dabble in property and occasionally sell a home. But they don't own much property themselves and really don't have a handle on how buying and selling for investment is done. The worst thing about these agents is that they will give you advice gleaned from their own experience, usually *bad* advice!

Willing to Work with You.   The right agent will quickly realize that you're sincere about investing and will also realize that if he or she plays their cards right, you'll buy multiple properties through them over a period of many years. In short, they'll understand that you represent a renewable resource. Hence, they'll be willing to assist you, show you properties over many months, suggest courses of action, and so forth. In other words, they'll be interested in a long-term relationship.

Where should I look for the "right" agent?

Of course, start by checking out the oldest agency in town as noted above. Then, locate a franchise office within the area in which you want to buy. (Remember, one of your first tasks is to identify your "farm" or locale where you'll buy.) Be sure to go to that office, not another branch of the same company. Ask to speak to the broker. Each office is usually organized with a broker/manager and a number of salespeople. The broker is the one who runs the show. However, if you just come in and ask to speak to an "agent" (a generic term that can mean either broker or salesperson), you'll get the next person "up." This is the salesperson who's on duty today, often a beginner. Once you get this person, you'll be stuck with him or her. (You'll have trouble switching because agents don't like stepping on the toes of their associates and "stealing" prospects.) Explain exactly what you're looking for: the most experienced agent in the office to help you get started investing long term. Explain you don't want a hot shot. You want someone who has the time to explain the business to you. (It could very well be the very broker you're talking to. However, brokers who run offices rarely have the time to spend on first-time investors. More likely it's another broker who's "parked" his or her license there.)

How do I interview the agent?

When you "hire" an agent, it's similar to hiring anyone else to work for you. You should interview them by asking them a series of questions to see if they have the experience and knowledge that you need and if they are compatible with you. Some questions you may want to ask are:

1. How long have you been active in the business of selling real estate (not just investing on your own)? How many properties did you sell last year? Remember, five years or more in the business is a good answer. At least half a dozen sales is also a good sign.
2. Do you invest on you own? If so, how many properties do you currently have? More than 5 is a good answer. More than 10 is better.

3. Would you be willing to work with me/us over the long haul? (A wise broker will wait to answer this until he or she has had time to *interview you* and see just how much of an investor you are!)

Should I work with one agent or several?

Is it better to work with one agent or with several? The answer is, "It depends." When you're first starting out, my suggestion is that you find one good agent (as explained above) and stick with him or her like glue. Your loyalty to the agent will be paid off by loyalty to you and advice and help that you really need. However, once you've become an experienced investor, then you may want to work with several different agents. Of course, you won't expect the kind of loyalty or attention that you'd receive by working with one agent exclusively. However, by then you may not need it. When you're an advanced investor, you may want to work with a group of agents in order to have the best chance at finding a specific type of property. (With commercial, industrial, or apartment properties, sometimes agents will keep listings to themselves.) You'll let them know exactly what you're looking for in terms of property and that you're working with others. However, by then they should have confidence that you'll buy through whoever finds what you want. You'll also let them know you'll pay a buyer's commission, if necessary, for their efforts. This will help ensure that they continue to look for properties that you can use and call you when they find them. Remember that most agents value loyalty above all else. The worst insult you can give an agent is letting him or her spend hours, days, weeks, and longer looking for property for you only to have you buy it through someone else. If you give an agent loyalty—work exclusively through them—very often they will reward you with superior service. However, when it comes to investment property, agents also realize that investors are looking for something special that they may not have. They realize that investors will work with several different agents trying to find the right property. Although they won't spend a lot of dedicated time looking just for you, if what you want happens to show up, they'll be happy to tell you about it, show it to you, sell it, and claim a commission.

Can I ask an agent to cut the commission?

Most good agents will ask a minimum commission below which they will not work. They may say, for example, that they are worth a full 3 percent (the half of a 6 percent commission that a seller's or buyer's agent usually gets) and they don't want to work for less. It's important to understand that there is no "set" or "fixed" or "standard" commission in real estate. If you then badger them to cut their rate, you're asking them to work for less than they feel they are worth. Some honest agents will simply refuse. They know their value. Others may grudgingly acquiesce, but you may have poisoned the relationship between you. They will surely resent what you did, and then you'll always be wondering if they are doing as good a job as they should. My advice is to do one of two things if you want to pay less. First, of course, find out how much the agent wants. Then, either agree to the amount or find another agent who is willing to work for less and tells you so right up front.

Should I work with a "buyer's agent"?

This is almost essential if you're going to be successful as an investor. However, be sure you know the difference between a "buyer's agent" versus a "seller's agent." An agent must declare who she or he works for. There are three options: the seller, the buyer, or both (called a "dual" agency). This has nothing to do with who pays the agent. It is perfectly acceptable for the seller to pay an agent who works for the buyer. In fact, it's done all the time. The reason it's important for you to use a buyer's agent (when you're purchasing property) is because there are issues involved. If the agent declares for you, then he or she has a fiduciary responsibility to you. This agent is supposed to look out for your interests. Sometimes, agents will declare that they are dual, that is, that they work for both parties. Most buyers will accept this; but to my way of thinking, this is not acceptable. A dual agent is neither fish nor fowl. He or she often can't fully represent you without hurting the seller and vice-versa. Thus, the dual agent often ends up trying to shepherd a deal through without anyone's really getting hurt. The unfortunate result for you, the buyer, is that you're not likely to get what you want—a bargain! In almost all states, an agent must declare whom he or she represents in writing. While this can be done at any time before an offer is made, it most certainly should be done at the time you decide to fill out a purchase agreement. And it must be done in writing. (Be sure you save the document. It could come in handy later on if the agent does something harmful to your cause.) Some excellent agents are able to handle the dual role. But for my money, I'd go with a buyer's agent any day.

Do I have to pay the buyer's agent?

It depends. Usually a buyer's agent splits the commission with the seller's agent. This happens when the selling agent co-brokers or cooperates on the listing. Sometimes, however, the seller's agent will refuse to co-broker. As noted, this occasionally happens in bigger investments such as apartment buildings, commercial, or industrial properties. This means that the seller's agent will want the entire commission, or at least a bigger share of it. In that case, you might, indeed, need to pay your buyer's agent a commission, or a portion of it. However, in this circumstance the deal will, hopefully, be big enough and with enough profit for you that you won't mind. Be wary when a buyer's agent asks you to sign an agency agreement. Be sure it does not lock you into paying a commission if the agent can get it from the other side. (You don't want the agent to collect twice, once from the seller and again from you!) You also don't want to make it too easy to get the commission from you (easier than arguing with the seller's agent for it). Also, be sure you're not liable for a commission or fee if you *don't* buy and that the agreement has a definite termination date. And, check to see whether it allows you to work with other agents, or requires you to work exclusively with one.

Do I want to work with discount agents?

When it's time to sell your investment property, you surely won't want to pay anymore than necessary in commission. If that's the case, you'll want to consider two alternatives: selling it on your own or selling through a discount broker. Today there are agents in almost all com-

DO YOU HAVE A GOOD AGENT?

munities who will work on a discount basis, some with very steep discounts. That means that *selling* agents will work for as little as 1 percent (instead of the selling agent's typical 3 percent commission). Keep in mind, however, that these agents are not likely to be the sort who you want and need when you first start investing. The reason is that these discounters sometimes compensate for a lower commission by providing a lesser service. If you're going to use a discount broker, be sure you get in writing exactly the services that will be performed. And be sure that these are what you want . . . and need.

QUESTIONS TO ASK YOUR AGENT

What is your specialty?

This is a legitimate question. And you should expect a candid reply. If the agent's specialty is single-family houses and condos, don't expect him or her to turn up any good deals in office buildings for you. Or in commercial, industrial, or land either. That's the reason you may eventually need to work with a variety of agents. Find a good one who specializes in commercial, for example; another in bare land and farms; and so on. In this way, you'll be able to diversify your portfolio of real estate holdings slowly. Keep in mind, however, that when you're first getting started, the easiest route is by buying homes and condos. Thus, your first agent should be one who works with investors in that area.

How long have you worked in real estate as an agent?

You're dealing with the agent to benefit from his or her knowledge and experience. You don't want the agent to be so green as to be learning from you. Beware of the agent who wants to strike up a bargain with you on the basis that you're both just starting out. It can sound very appealing. You'll learn together. It will be a shared experience. You'll both be on the same path to riches as you acquire property. As I said, it sounds good. However, it doesn't really make any sense. In truth, a green agent and a green investor are like the blind leading the blind. You're prepared to pay a fair commission to the agent. In return, you should expect advice born of experience. Anything less and you're wasting your time and money. Ideally the agent will tell you that he or she has worked in real estate for 20 years or more. For an investor, my suggestion is that any agent with fewer than 5 years of full-time experience is just getting started. I know that agents who have fewer than 5 years and are reading this will likely argue with my suggestion. Nevertheless, there are many occupant home buyers for beginning agents to learn from. And once the agent has had a chance to go through many deals and become experienced, he or she can begin acquiring savvy investors such as you as clients.

How do you feel about other agents in your field?

This is really a trick question, and one of my favorites. (I have never seen anyone else suggest asking it.) It has to do with human nature. My experience has been that someone who is really good at what they do will rarely knock a competitor. Rather, this person will be big enough to understand that others are trying hard and may be less (or sometimes more) successful. This agent will be comfortable with his or her success and not try to enhance it at the expense of others. Therefore, my idea of a good agent is one who simply says that most other agents that he or she knows work hard and try to do a good job . . . and leave it at that. Beware of the agent who tries to demean competitors with comments such as, "Jane just isn't in my league," or "Peter does a terrible job and won't find you a good property," or "Poor Sally is really a joke amongst other brokers," or "I can't believe you'd consider working with poor Harry—he just doesn't work hard for his clients." A solid agent will promote himself or herself, not try to win your confidence by demeaning others. It isn't professional. It's sign of poor judgment. And it should be a red flag warning to you.

How many properties do you own?

This is definitely not a question you'd ask of an agent whom you were asking to find you a house in which to live. Why would you care how many properties such an agent owned? On the other hand, as an investor, you want to know that your agent is an investor too. You want to know that your agent intimately understands the techniques and problems of working with tenants; that he or she knows how to put a commercial property deal together; that the agent is comfortable handling the type of real estate in which you want to invest. My own personal feeling is that owning at least 10 properties is reasonable, particularly if the agent specializes in single-family residential units. If the agent specializes in commercial or apartment buildings, then 5 might be appropriate. If the agent, of course, has only been in business for 5 years or so, the number will undoubtedly be much less. On the other hand, if you're dealing with an agent with 20 years of experience, expect him or her to own a lot of real estate. After all, that's the agent's chosen profession, and acquired property is the name of the game.

How often do you come across good deals?

Expect a wry smile at this question. An experienced agent knows that "steals"—properties that can be bought for a fraction of their true value—are usually few and far between. On the other hand, there are often many solid deals where a savvy investor can pick up a good property for a reasonable price and, over a period of years, turn it into a cash cow. A good answer would be, "Yes, every so often I come across an exceptional deal. However, in between there are many good opportunities that I can show you in which you stand to make a healthy profit." It's very likely an honest answer. Beware of the agent who says, "I have access to deals that no one else in the area has. I can show you properties on which you can make a fortune overnight." Sound too good to be true? If so, then it probably is. No one is going to show you how to pick up money that's lying in the streets. If it were, they'd pick it up themselves.

Do you have an investment group?

Savvy agents often form partnerships or simply associations of investors in order to purchase more and/or larger properties. These investment groups are great for the agent, since they provide an opportunity for a quick sale and commission when a good deal arises. They are also great for the investors who get to share in a lot of different opportunities. However, usually a savvy agent will only let in those investors whom he or she trusts and who is ready to buy when a good deal crops up. If your agent has investment groups, you should ask if you can join. If the agent immediately says, "Yes," be wary. The group may be nothing more than a sham on which the agent dumps unprofitable properties. Be more interested if the agent suggests that after he or she and you have worked together on a few deals, he or she will let you know. A savvy agent will want to take as much stock of you as you want to take of him or her.

Is it your policy to buy first for yourself?

You don't want any agent who buys all the good properties for himself or herself and leaves the tailings for you. Contrary to what many newcomers believe, a good agent will usually present the best deals to his or her clients. That provides the agent with a steady stream of cash from commissions. And positive cash flow is one of the hardest and most important things to get in real estate. Be wary of an agent who says, "Of course, I *always* save the very best properties for my clients." No one is that altruistic. A savvy agent will certainly present some of the best to his or her clients. But that agent will also pick some cherries for himself or herself.

11

Is It a True Fixer-Upper?

QUESTIONS TO ASK YOURSELF

Is it really a fixer-upper?

☐

There are as many definitions of what constitutes a fixer-upper (also called a "handyman special") as there are people who want to jump in and buy one, presumably at a deep discount. For example, many people feel a fixer-upper refers only to homes. Others consider other types of property as well, such as apartment buildings, commercial units, and so on. Some people feel any property that's not in top shape constitutes a fixer-upper. For example, I remember one buyer who, when shown a home, would comment that the paint had a few blemishes and there were a couple of spots on the carpet—hence it was a fixer-upper and she expected the sellers immediately to knock 15 percent off the price. Of course, in a hot market such as we've seen recently, it was more likely she'd end up paying full price or better to get such a property, rather than the other way around. To my way of thinking, a fixer-upper is a property with serious problems. These problems take many forms. And you can expect to negotiate a much deeper discount when you buy.

Why do I want a fixer-upper?

☐

There can be several different reasons. Some people love to work on houses, your author being one of them. It poses a challenge to come in and take what is essentially a wreck, fix it up into a very polished home, and resell for a profit. That leads to the second motive, profit. Many investors feel there's money to be made in fixer-uppers. Indeed, I've known investors whose exclusive business was to renovate run-down properties. And some of them made a handsome living at it. Yet another reason is to help you get into an area you couldn't otherwise afford. It may be that in today's market your first choice of area is simply unattainable unless you can get a home at a deep discount. A fixer-upper offers that possibility. You might very well be able to buy a fixer-upper for significantly less than similar homes in the neighborhood are selling for, move in, and then over time fix it up into a splendid home.

Will I need to live in the fixer-upper?

I can tell you from painful experience that it's difficult, if not sometimes impossible, to live in the same property you're fixing up. Yet, that is just what many fixer-uppers hope to do. By moving in, you save on paying twice for mortgage/rent, utilities, and all the other costs of operating two properties. By living in the home you can cut your living costs substantially. That's the up side. The down side is that you will be eternally surrounded by dust, paint smells, debris, workers, noise, and all the other things that go along with a worksite. You'll find that you'll be forced to get up early in the morning because that's when workers like to get started. You may have to convert a bathroom into a kitchen while the existing kitchen is being remodeled. Or you may be reduced to one bathroom instead of two or more. (Health and safety codes normally prohibit inhabiting a property where there is no working bathroom and kitchen.) Further, you'll find that no matter what you're working on fixing up, your living situation (clothing, pots, pans, dishes, foodstuffs, TV, and so on) is in the way—and vice versa. In short, if you're planning to save money by moving in while doing the work, be prepared for a "living hell" as one fixer-upper entrepreneur I knew described it. Be sure your family situation is solid. Living and working on a fixer-upper can strain a relationship. And be absolutely sure that it's the sort of thing you want to do.

Can I do the work myself?

In most cases, the answer is yes, it's possible for you to do it yourself. (In some areas, building codes require the electrical, plumbing, gas, and other utility work be done by licensed contractors.) The real questions are: Do you want to? and How much do you want to do? For the inexperienced, refurbishing a home can be hard work and the results may not always be what you anticipate. For example, something as apparently elementary as hooking up the plumbing for a sink, dishwasher, and garbage disposal can require getting on the floor and climbing into small confined spaces, making fittings that actually don't leak, lifting fairly heavy appliances, and so on. And this may only be the finishing touch. There's also replacing, fixing, or painting/staining cabinets, replacing a countertop, and putting in new electrical and plumbing outlets. In a truly major fix-up, the work can be daunting. It can include lifting the entire home off its foundation on hydraulic jacks, digging out the old cement foundation, and pouring new. It can mean getting up on a roof and replacing old shingles. It might mean busting out Sheetrock and framing and replacing walls entirely. I've done all of these things, and I can tell you, while it's rewarding work, it's not something everyone can or should tackle. It's very important to be realistic about doing work yourself on a fixer-upper. You need to ask experts exactly what's involved, how much effort and skill it takes, and then make a decision as to whether you can do it and want to do it. Keep in mind that if you do decide to push forward, there's the matter of how it will turn out. A first-timer doing plaster work is very likely to create a botched job. The same holds true for almost any of the building trade work. My own feeling is that if you lack both skill and experience, build into your plan funds to cover the cost of having professionals do the work.

Do I know the three rules for success with fixer-uppers?

Every fixer-upper job must abide by at least three rules to be successful. If you violate these rules, you'll find that while you may do your level best, you'll come out a loser. And that's not something any of us wants to be. Here are the three rules for success when working with fixer-uppers:

1. *Buy Low.* This is probably the most critical. If you buy right, you'll have enough margin to fix up the

property and sell it for a profit. If you buy wrong, no matter how much money you try to save by cutting corners, it will be a money loser.

2. *Cut Costs.*   If you're the sort of person who plans to hire out every little thing, if you don't know people in the building industry who will cut you deals, if you pay retail for everything you purchase, chances are you'll lose money on a fixer-upper. In order to be successful, you have to be able to contain your fixing-up costs.

3. *Be Quick.*   Time works against you when you're fixing up a property. If it's a rental, that's rent lost during the fix-up period. In addition, there are the carrying costs. These include mortgage, taxes, insurance, utilities, and so on. They come due every month regardless of how long you take. And over time they can turn a profit margin into a loss.

Do I understand how to buy property low?

It's important to grasp that successful fixer-uppers are people who use a formula, simple though it may be, when buying their properties. They don't deviate from this formula even a little bit. If they did, they'd lose money. The formula is quite simple:

Purchase price = Resale price – (profit + carrying costs + fix-up costs + transaction fees)

To understand this formula, you need to work backwards. You start off with the price you hope to resell for plus the costs of the sale such as a commission, escrow, and title fees. You should be able to get a close estimate of the *transaction costs* from any broker. You can get the *fix-up costs* in a variety of ways. Some experienced in this arena can make the call themselves. If you're less experienced, you should call in professionals to give you bids. The more accurate your estimates, the better. *Carrying costs* should be fairly accurate, depending on your timeline. You should know how much it costs for mortgage payment, taxes, insurance, utilities, and so on for one month. Multiply that by the number of months it will take you to complete the job. Then there's the *profit*. How much do you want/need to make? Finally, when you've added all these items together, you subtract them from the resale price—how much you can get for the property when you resell. You can get a *resale price* by looking at properties similar to yours that have already been fixed up.

Have I compensated for a future price?

Don't forget to "forward price," that is, to add to the potential sales price whatever homes happen to be appreciating for at the time—keeping in mind, of course, that past appreciation is no guarantee of the future. (For example, if prices are going up 10 percent a year and you figure it will take a year to do the job, add 10 percent to the potential resale price, then follow the formula detailed above.) The result is what you should pay for the fixer-upper. You may find that it's a startlingly low price, far less than the seller is asking. Whoa, you may say to yourself. I'll never get the property for that price. No, then move on. There will be other, better properties. If you pay even a few dollars more, it will have to come out of somewhere . . . and chances it will be your profit.

Can I cut fixing costs?

Of course, when faced with the fact that you can't buy a property for what you need to pay in order to be successful as a fixer-upper, many people will look for a sharper pencil. Where can they trim costs? Reselling price, transaction fees (unless you sell by owner and not use a broker—which may or may not work), carrying costs and the profit you hope to make usually are intractable. (Yes, you can cut your profit, but then why go through all the trouble.) The one area where costs can be cut is in the fix-up process itself. Can you buy wholesale instead of retail? Possibly, if you're working with a builder and use his or her name to get better deals from building supply houses. Can you cut costs by doing some of the work yourself? Yes, certainly, but reread the question above on doing the work yourself. Further, keep in mind that even if you do the work yourself, your time isn't (or shouldn't be) free. How much do you make at your "day job?" You should add that in as a cost for time spent on the fixer. If you spend 500 hours working on the project and your regular wage is $35 an hour, that's $17,500. Don't add it in and you've done a lot of work, and lost a lot of money.

___

Do I have a realistic timeline?

When doing any kind of construction work, the basic rule is that everything takes longer (and costs more) than estimated. For one thing, there's waiting time. You've called in a plumber to change out some cast iron piping for copper piping. The job is costing you $10,000. You really can't start much of anything else until the plumbing is done because it requires ripping out some walls, working under the house and in the attic, and having the water turned off. The plumber says he will be there on Thursday. But, he's a no-show. Then it's Friday, then a week, then three weeks. Frantically you call the plumber—what gives, you ask? The plumber is apologetic, but explains that another job is taking longer than planned. He'll be out tomorrow and sure enough, he arrives! He spends one day taking out the old plumbing and then disappears for more weeks. When called, he explains he's got other jobs to finish. Multiply this by almost every workman you call out. Yes, some in the trades are able to keep to a strict schedule. But in my experience, many take on multiple jobs at the same time. They need to do this to keep constantly busy. And as a result, things tend to fall behind. True, you can get a tradesperson to sign a contract with a set start and finish date and penalties for late work. But, chances are that sort of contract will cost you top dollar, not the kind of cost cutting you hope to achieve. All of which says that you must build a lot of air into your timeline. If you figure it will take you a month to fix up the house, plan for three. If you figure it will take you three months, plan for nine. If you're lucky and you get it done on time, or close to on time, terrific. But, if things drag out, you won't find that you've turned your profit into loss by not packing enough time into the deal.

QUESTIONS TO ASK THE SELLER

Will you accept a realistic offer?

Sellers rarely understand fixer-upper pricing. They see that homes similar to theirs are selling for $400,000 in their area. They know they've got some repair problems, so they knock $10,000 off the price and hope to sell. You, on the other hand, after going through the formula noted above, realize that you can't pay more than $200,000 for the property—almost 50 percent less than they are asking. Will they accept such a lowball proposition? You'll never know until you ask. My suggestion is that you come in with all your calculation and show the seller exactly how you arrived at your price. If you were realistic, so too may be the seller. However, keep in mind that some other entrepreneur looking for a fixer-upper may not have heard about the formula and may offer the seller $350,000. Of course, the seller will accept and you'll be out. But when (not if) that happens, don't feel bad. Just think of the loss that pie-eyed entrepreneur is going to take when he or she finally adds up all the costs and tries to resell for a profit!

Will you co-fix-up with me?

Don't overlook the possibility of making the seller into a partner. Sellers who blanch at the prospect of selling their home for far below what they consider a good price might be happy to reconsider for a 25 percent interest in the fixing-up deal. Of course, point out that in order to be a partner, they must participate in the costs of the fix-up. If they hesitate at that, point out that a percentage of the costs can be subtracted from their potential profits. Sometimes when faced with the realities of what it will cost to fix up a home, the seller may see that it's simpler just to sell at your offered price. This is particularly the case if there haven't been any other offers in a long time. Just be sure that you've done your homework and that the costs you've put down are realistic. Nothing will sour a deal faster than for the seller to call up a plumber or carpenter, get them out to the property, and get a bid that's a fraction of the cost you've estimated.

Have you disclosed all the problems with the property?

With a fixer, it's very important to know just what you're getting into. That means close scrutiny of the seller's disclosure and a thorough professional home inspection on your part. That home inspection may be quite elaborate, involving visits by a variety of inspectors including roofers, structural and soil engineers, and more—be sure your purchase agreement provides for this. But even more, you want to be sure that your inspectors haven't overlooked, and the seller failed to disclose, some critical factor. Remember, the inspectors can only report on what they see, not on what's hidden. And a seller who's lived in a property for many years may know of some important defect that's not apparent. For example, years ago a structural beam in the center of the home may have cracked because of termite damage. Instead of being replaced, it was merely shored up with a couple of small supporting beams. It's lasted all this time, but may be ready to collapse at any time in the future. However, it's hidden. Inspectors haven't caught it. And the seller neglected to mention it on her disclosures. Now you ask the seller if there's anything more. You point out that you'll be refurbishing many parts of the property. Anything hidden will come out. And you'd hate to get involved in a lawsuit over something that should have been disclosed and wasn't. You might also point out that records of things such as termite clearances and previous inspection reports and work are usually available and go back many years. Upon second thought, perhaps the seller might mention that bad beam. Now you have your clue. You get a new inspection on it. And perhaps save yourself $10,000 or more in added costs. It never hurts to ask.

12

Do You Know What's Involved in Being a Landlord?

QUESTIONS TO ASK YOURSELF

What is a good tenant?

Good tenants are usually defined by most landlords as people who pay their rent on time, don't damage the property, and don't complain too much. How do you find such tenants? The trick is to check them out *before* you rent. But this can be tricky. You have to tread carefully to avoid a minefield of Fair Housing Laws (discussed below). However, you can ask financial questions of tenants. After all, you're entrusting them with a huge financial investment—your house.

Should I use a rental application?

You should provide every potential tenant with a thorough rental application. (These are available in books that specialize in renting as well as from agents and attorneys.) The application should include permission for you to run a credit check, contact current employers, and call previous landlords. You should do all three things. Start with a credit report. No, don't expect that all of your tenants will have sterling credit. But you should expect to find a history of making payments on time. If the applicant is always paying his or her bills late, it doesn't bode well for timely rent payments. You can get a credit report by contacting a local credit bureau. You can also have a local real estate agent run one for you. (Remember, you must have the applicant's permission to do this.)

Should I actually call previous landlords? □

Yes, provided the application the would-be tenant signs gives you permission. Perhaps even more important than calling the current landlord is to check with the tenant's previous landlords. (If this is a bad tenant, the current landlord may give you a wonderful report just to get rid of the tenant!) You probably won't get many details, as landlords are wary of saying anything that could get them into a lawsuit with tenants. But they will usually let you know if they would be willing to rent to the tenant again. If not, then you might want to skip this tenant as well.

Should I actually call the tenant's current employer? □

With the tenant's permission, you can contact the tenant's current employer and ask to verify the employment and the income. Confirming that the tenant told the truth on the application will make you look more favorably upon him or her and help satisfy you that the tenant will have the income to handle the rent.

Can I handle rentals by myself? □

Yes, you certainly can. However, you must operate from a position of knowledge. You must know what federal and state laws say you can and can't do, particularly when it comes to antidiscrimination laws (see below). And you must know many of the tricks of the trade that good landlords follow. I suggest you read up on landlording. There are a number of good books on the market that can help you. Of course, I suggest my own: *The Landlord's Trouble Shooter*, Third Edition (Dearborn, 2004). Here's a partial list of some of the things that many investor/landlords do entirely on their own:

Handle Repairs. Of course, you must do all repairs in a safe and workmanlike manner. Replacing a faucet washer is easy. Working with gas or electricity is difficult and to avoid liability issues, you may want to call in a professional. Note: some areas require work on gas, electric and other utilities be done only be professionals.

Find Good Tenants.   As the owner of the property, you are in the best position to judge how good a tenant is likely to be. (See above for clues on finding good tenants.) If you hire out the job to a property management firm, it's likely to cost you upwards of 11 to 12 percent of your rental income.

Perform Ongoing Maintenance.   To save money, you can come by once a week to mow the lawns, service the pool/spa, and clean up around the property. But most landlords prefer to hire out these tasks.

Rent-up.   Most landlords advertise, talk to prospective tenants, check out their credit, call previous landlords—but do it all within the law. Get permission for checks from the tenants and observe antidiscrimination rules when advertising and renting-up.

Deal with Tenants' Complaints.   You're "the boss" here. If not you, who else will deal with the complaints? Handle them promptly.

Collect Rent.   Unless you hire a property management firm, you should go down and collect the rent. With good tenants, you can have them mail it in. With slow-paying tenants, you may have to go down and pick it up. A physical presence on your part helps keep things running smoothly.

Do I understand fair housing laws?

Fair housing laws are national and, in many cases, local in scope. If you're a landlord, it's your responsibility to know and understand them. A good place to start is by joining the National Apartment Association, www.naahq.org. Most major cities also have local organizations of landlords. They can keep you up to date on antidiscrimination laws. You'll also want to check out the Fair Housing Act of 1988. It created a number of protected classes against whom you cannot discriminate when advertising or renting most properties. (There are some exceptions.) The protected classes include: color, race, religion, national origin or ancestry, sex, familial status, and physical disability. Also, the Americans with Disabilities Act (ADA) provides that you must allow additional rights to tenants to, for example, keep a companion animal when prescribed by a physician, or offer a parking space close to a mobility-impaired tenant. Keep in mind that these antidiscrimination rules in many cases apply when you're advertising, offering to show, and negotiating, as well as actually renting. Severe penalties are imposed if you fail to follow the rules. For more information, you can get a free brochure from HUD through its Fair Housing Information Clearinghouse, www.hud.gov.

Do I have to give the tenant disclosures?

Probably. The federal government mandates that you provide most tenants with a lead disclosure statement regarding any lead in the property. You may also want to provide disclosures on asbestos, black mold, and other contaminants or toxic agents that could be in the property. This could help you later on should the tenants get sick and claim it's your fault. Check with your attorney.

Do I need to provide smoke detectors in rentals?

Absolutely, in all jurisdictions I know of. In some areas you will also need to provide carbon monoxide detectors as well as fire extinguishers. Your rental agreement should specify what you have provided, and the tenants should acknowledge that they have seen these and understand their use.

Where can I get a rental agreement?

Many landlords' associations will provide you with one. Real estate agents may also have rental agreements they can let you use. But, since it forms the basis of your relationship with your tenant(s), you should always have any rental agreement form checked over by a good attorney. Remember, the rental agreement should specify not only the amount of the rent and where it's to be paid, but everything you expect from the tenant—and what the tenant can expect from you. Don't shirk on getting a good rental agreement. It can make or break your landlording experience.

How much rent can I charge?

Unless you're in one of the dwindling number of rent control areas (about which you should query the agent, the seller, and local government), you can charge as much as you want. However, it's important to keep in mind that you won't get more than the market warrants. Just as when properties are for sale, when units are for rent you must accede to the demand and the competition (supply). In every neighborhood, there are likely to be many rental properties. And you're in competition with all of them. Homes that are bigger than yours with more amenities (such as a pool, spa, tennis court, or whatever) will command higher rents. Those that are smaller, more poorly located, and not as clean will get a lower rent. But somewhere in between is a maximum rent that you can charge. Tenants shop around and they know what a given property should rent for. Try to get much above market, and your property will sit there unrented for months. (Getting it rented-up as quickly as possible is the first order of business—vacancies are very costly.) My suggestion is that for a few weekends you become a pretend tenant. Go around to your competition. See what they have to offer and what they are charging. Very quickly you'll see where your property fits in and how much rent you can charge. (Actually, if you can do this *before* you buy, it's even better. That way you get a clearer picture of your property's true income potential.) I would suggest that to rent-up the property quickly, you charge slightly below market. The money you'll save over the long haul in having your property rented continuously will more than make up for the few dollars less a month you get.

When can I raise rents?

You can only raise rents when the rental market justifies it. When the economy in your area improves, the demand for housing increases and shortages of rental property occur. When the supply/demand warrants it, you can raise your rents. Most landlords wait to raise the rents significantly until a tenant moves out and a new one moves in.

Should I raise an existing tenant's rent?

Raising an existing tenant's rent risks losing that tenant, unless the market warrants it. Keep in mind that sometimes you can actually raise your rents for an existing tenant to slightly above the market rate due to inertia. Once a tenant is in your unit, it's hard for that tenant to move out. There's the hassle of finding a new apartment, of dealing with the movers, of changing the utilities, mail, and phone, and on and on. In other words, all things being equal, tenants who are basically happy with where they live would rather not move if they could choose not to do so. So when you raise the rent, they'll comparison shop. If you charge only a small amount above market, they may figure it's easier to pay than to move. You should avoid big rent increases because they unnerve existing tenants and make them more likely to jump ship. Also, try to do something for the tenant, such as repainting or recarpeting, before you raise the rent. My own feeling is that if you have a good tenant, you should honor that person by keeping the rents low and refurbishing the place on a regular basis. It'll keep the tenant happy. And it'll save you the very large amount of money involved in rerenting.

How big a deposit should I demand?

The straight answer is, as big as possible. That may not be as big as you want. Some states impose maximum limits on cleaning/security deposits—often one and a half to two times the monthly rent. Further, in some states you may be required to keep any deposit money in a trust account that pays interest. When the tenant moves out, you may owe back not only the deposit, but interest on it as well. In addition, you may be limited by the marketplace. If all the landlords around you are charging one month's rent as a deposit, you'll have trouble charging two. Further, coming up with more than a month's deposit may be a hardship for many tenants. This is particularly the case when you're insisting on a lease with first and last months' rent up front. That could mean the equivalent of three or four months' rent paid to you by a tenant. Keep in mind that the purpose of the deposit is to help insure that the tenant takes good care of the property. It's both an incentive and a deterrent. Your message to the tenant is: Keep the place clean, and you'll get your money back. Make a mess, and you'll lose it. Usually one to one and a half months' rent is sufficient to make the point. However, you may want to charge extra deposits for such things as pets, waterbeds, and so on.

What should I do to prepare a property for tenants?

Dirty and messy properties take far longer to rent, command lower rents, and attract a much lower quality tenant. The person you really hurt when you fail to clean up your rental is you. Therefore, I always go through a rental and clean the carpets and floors and make sure the kitchen is spotless, with the stove, refrigerator (if any), and sink shiny and clean. I also repaint the walls as necessary. When prospective tenants walk in, I want them to think they are getting a place that's as good as new. That way, hopefully, they'll take pride in living there and will take care of it. You have to be careful of properties that get a tired look. Sometimes when a property has a lot of tenants moving through it, it begins to take on a shabby appearance. After a while the landlord tires of spending the money and time to clean it thoroughly after each move-out. When that happens, it's the start of a death spiral. Each successive tenant will be worse than the previous one. And after each increasingly quick move-out, the place will look worse. The solution is a complete makeover. Spend the bucks to put the property back in top shape so that you can attract a top tenant. Remember, a good tenant simply won't accept a rental that's a mess. And that tenant won't want to do your job of cleaning.

Should I pay for utilities?

That depends on your circumstances. If you routinely pay for utilities, expect that tenants will assume it's covered in their rent and may not hesitate to run the water or the heat excessively. With the high costs of fuels today, your utility bills in a hot summer or cold winter could actually come close to matching your entire rental income! A better way of handling it is to have the tenant pay for most of the utilities. If necessary, you can reduce the rent slightly to accommodate this. The tenant who pays his or her own utilities is more likely to pay attention to being economical. There are, of course, exceptions. In some multiunit buildings there are no separate meters. In this situation, you might be able to bill the tenants separately each month: get the utility bill and divide it among all of the renters. This, however, is not a great answer as you're likely to get lots of complaining. Another exception has to do with water. If you live in a hot climate, you'll probably want to pay the water bill, or else the tenant, in striving to reduce costs, may forget to water your landscaping. Don't expect any tenant to go out of his or her way to pay a big water bill to help your garden. Another answer is a water allowance. It doesn't have to be much. It doesn't even have to equal the costs the tenant will pay for all water actually used. It's just the idea that you're contributing. Each time the tenant thinks about not watering, he or she may remember that allowance and not get angry about the cost and water. Another utility sometimes worth paying is garbage collection. I've had tenants who, to save money, never signed up for this service, instead occasionally hauling their garbage to the dump. This can become a health hazard and cleanliness issue. Since the garbage is usually a fixed, small amount each month, sometimes it's simply easier if you, the landlord, pay it.

Should I restrict pets?

Pets are wonderful. All my life I've had either dogs or cats as pets and loved them all. But they can be hard on a rental. The biggest problem (besides dogs barking) is urination. Animals really don't have the same understanding as human beings do when it comes to urinating. While some will hold it in for as much as a day until you let them out, others will let nature take its course. For you as a landlord, urine problems on the floor can be a nightmare. Regardless of what some products claim to do, I've never found any product that could remove the odor. And the stain often will go down through carpets, through padding, and sometimes even into cement and wood floors! The cost of recarpeting after a pet has ruined a wall-to-wall carpeted rental can be many thousands of dollars. Hence, most landlords would prefer not to have pets.

Can I restrict pets?

Many tenants, some excellent ones, come with pets. But be wary if a would-be tenant says he or she will remove the pet. You can never be sure that a month or so after moving in, so too will the pet. One solution is to charge an extra deposit (where allowed) per pet. Even if it's only a few hundred dollars, many tenants will pay extra attention to their pets if they know it's going to cost them money. However, this only works if you convince the tenants that they will get the money back if the property is left clean and odorless when they leave. Note: You may be required to allow a companion pet when the tenant has a doctor's order for it.

Should I get a lease?

Many first-time investors think that the solution to a large number of rental problems is the lease. Get the tenant to sign a solid lease for six months, a year, or more and you can put that unit out of your mind. Unfortunately, that's often not the case. Residential tenants with a lease can still call you for every maintenance and repair problem, real or imagined. And because they have the lease, they'll expect you to fix it promptly. (If you fail to maintain the property in a reasonable manner, it could be a lease breaker for them.) Further, the lease is only as good as the tenant. If you have a year's lease and your tenant decides to move out after a month, your recourse is to sue that tenant each month as the rent comes due. If the tenant skips town and has no obvious assets, even suing can end up costing you money without the hope of getting anything back. In addition, you have a duty to mitigate the damages so that once the tenant is gone, you need to clean up the property and rerent it. And once it's rerented, you probably can't sue the tenant for lost rent, because someone else is paying it! Thus, many landlords will simply write off a bad tenant who skips out on a lease. Also, a lease may prevent you from raising rents or even selling. In a residential situation, you're probably locking in the rent for the term of the lease. Finally, if the tenants adhere to the terms of the lease, you probably can't get rid of them until the lease expires.

Should I use a month-to-month tenancy arrangement?

What many landlord/investors prefer (your author included) is the month-to-month tenancy. It can be terminated with a month's notice (sometimes two months depending on the state you're in and the situation) by either party. Thus, if the tenants want to leave, they have a way out. If you want to raise rents or get them out so you can sell, you have a way to do it. (The tenancy normally runs with the land. The next landlord must continue to honor the rental agreements you make.) Besides, even with a month-to-month arrangement, you can still get first and last month's rent up front plus a cleaning/security deposit, if desired.

How do I keep my good tenants?

Keep them happy. That includes not raising the rent very often. Many landlords will raise the rents every year or even every six months on a tenant who pays well and doesn't complain much. Thus the reward for being a good tenant becomes higher rent. And, as a result, the tenant moves out. A wise landlord will keep the rents modest in order to keep the good tenant. The wise landlord will also pay special attention to any good tenant's complaint. If it's a legitimate problem, the landlord will get it fixed, pronto. Finally, the savvy landlord will have a regular maintenance schedule for each rental unit. Every three years, for example, the units all get painted. Every six years, they get new carpeting. And so on. Thus, the tenant who stays a long time isn't penalized. Instead, on a periodic basis, the property is upgraded. That's going to make any tenant happy.

What should I do when there's a repair problem?

This is the bane of most small investors/landlords. You've just settled back in your lounge chair after a lovely dinner and are enjoying an after-dinner drink, when there's a phone call. It's a tenant. It's raining outside and there's a leak. Water is coming in the roof and getting on their bed. They want it fixed now. So what does a good landlord do? He or she promptly fixes it. If it can be handled right away, get someone out there to do it. If it's going to take a few days, call the tenant, explain the situation, and ask for their indulgence. Then, get it fixed as soon as possible. Don't let any repair problem fester and slip over time. If the property becomes uninhabitable, the tenant may move out without paying rent. In most states, if you don't fix the problem after the tenants have given you reasonable notice, they may have the right to fix it themselves (often in the most expensive way) and then subtract the costs from their next rent. Repair and maintenance problems are a fact of life when you have rental property. They go with the territory. And, as an investor, it's up to you to take care of them.

What should I do about late rent?

Collect it as soon as possible. Every day that rent is late eats up some of your security deposit. Talk to the tenants. Find out *why* the rent is late. Explain that a home is their most important obligation. If they want to keep it, they must pay their rent first. Sometimes a good talk will help. Also, consider imposing a penalty for late rent. It's a good idea to include it in every rental agreement you write. After a grace period of typically five days, the penalty is usually $50 or 5 percent of the rent, whichever is smaller. In today's world, we are all conditioned to watch out for money penalties, and tenants are no different. You'd be surprised how careful they will be to get the rent in on time to avoid the penalty. Just be sure to enforce the clause.

What if a tenant refuses to pay me a late penalty?

If the tenant offers to give you the rent that is late, but balks over the penalty, you may want to refuse to accept the late rent until it includes the penalty. This runs the risk of not getting any rent. On the one hand, having once paid a penalty for late rent, the tenant probably will pay on time ever after. On the other hand, sometimes a carrot works better than a stick. You can try raising the rent and then giving a discount if it's paid on time. The rent for all tenants goes up by $100. But, if it's paid on or before the due date, a $100 discount applies. You'd be surprised how promptly most rents will come in. Of course, sometimes the tenant simply can't or won't pay. If it's a situation beyond the tenant's control (loss of employment, illness, and so on), you may actually want to help the tenant to move to friends or relatives. If it's simply an adamant tenant who refuses without giving a reason, or won't accept your help, then eviction may be the answer.

How do I evict a tenant?

Get an attorney. In all states, eviction can only be accomplished through judicial means. You'll need to get an "unlawful detainer" action through court. In many areas, it will cost you around $1,500 the first time. It will also take about a month. (Most judges will not give you an eviction until the tenant has used up all the security deposit in lieu of rent.) After you've done it one or two times, you may find that it's not that difficult and you can save money by acting as your own attorney. Many landlords do this regularly.

What should I do about a tenant who destroys or changes things?

Your rental agreement should spell out what a tenant can and can't do. If a tenant destroys or changes things without your written permission, you should immediately intervene. That means drawing the tenant's attention to the problem and insisting that it be corrected. In some cases involving health and safety, you may want to correct the situation yourself and then deduct the cost from the deposit and insist that the tenant then add to the deposit to bring it up to its previous level. In other cases, you may want to insist that the tenants themselves bring the changes back to the way things were. If it's a serious case of destruction, such as putting holes in walls, breaking appliances and fixtures, or causing fires, you may want to evict the tenant.

How often should I check up on my property?

During the first month of the tenancy, I like to check up a couple of times. Drop by and ask how the tenant is doing. Did the move-in go well? Is there anything you should know about or that needs fixing? You will need advance permission to go inside the property, unless it's an emergency, but you can simply drop by when the tenant is home to talk. Try to keep up good relations with the tenant. After the first month, I usually drop by once a month for three months to collect the rent and check out the place. After that, if it's a responsible tenant, I simply have them mail the rent in. But I still drive by at least once a month. It's your property and you need to know what's happening to it. Don't become an absentee landlord. You'll be the one who ends up paying the penalty.

Should I hire a property management firm?

You certainly can. They abound in almost every area of the country. Many real estate agents handle rentals as a sideline, hoping to develop listings from them. Keep in mind, however, that not all property management firms are run equally well. Some do a good job and others a poor one. Further, property management firms don't normally handle the maintenance and repairs themselves. Rather, they farm it out to professionals. So, in addition to the 11 to 12 percent fee the firm may charge for its administrative services, you may also find that you're getting socked for full-priced repair/maintenance costs. Most beginning investors/landlords prefer to do the property management themselves. It's a way to contain costs and to learn exactly what the business is all about.

QUESTIONS TO ASK TENANTS

Can I contact your previous landlord and do a credit check?

It's important to get this information as part of your screen process. You especially want to check with the landlord prior to the current one. (The current landlord may give you a glowing report just to get rid of a bad tenant!). Be sure you ask this question and get permission *in writing*. You don't want to have a tenant accuse you of invasion of privacy. Most landlords include it as part of their rental application.

How many pets do you have?

Pets, when uncontrolled, can do serious damage to a property. Over time, however, you'll find it's almost impossible to rent exclusively to tenants without pets. Therefore, you'll want to determine how many pets and what kind. You may want to set a separate cleaning deposit for each pet as a way of inducing your tenants to keep their animals under control. Remember, under the Americans with Disabilities Act, you must allow a tenant to have a seeing-eye dog. Also, a tenant has the right to have a companion animal as prescribed by a doctor. You cannot discourage a tenant from having a pet in these circumstances.

Do you have a waterbed?

Waterbeds, once the rage, are now much less common. Nevertheless, some tenants will have them, and they pose some concerns for landlords. The beds can be particularly heavy, and if you have an older building that wasn't constructed to modern standards, they can strain the structure. Further, if a waterbed pops, you can have water damage in the bedroom and possibly in rooms beneath. (Water damage can lead to black mold, which can be a real problem when renting or selling a property.) You may want to ask for a special security deposit from a tenant who has a waterbed.

How soon will you be able to move in?

Every day that your property is empty, you lose rent and have to pay expenses (including mortgage, taxes, utilities, and maintenance) out of your pocket. Therefore, finding a good tenant who wants to move in tomorrow is better than finding one who wants to move in next month. Most landlords give preferential treatment to tenants who can move in quickly. Sometimes, for a good tenant who wants to move in later, you may want to split the rent between the present and the move-in date.

How many people will occupy the property?

You will find it difficult to restrict the number of occupants, particularly children, in a rental. According to federal law you can't refuse to rent to families with children. However, some cities fighting high density in rental housing have their own rules that prohibit you from renting to more than a set number of people per unit. As a landlord, you're caught in the middle. At the least, find out the names and ages of each of the tenants who will occupy your property. You may want to argue that more than a certain number per bedroom is too many, but be sure you check with your attorney first.

How many cars do you own?

Usually rentals have limited parking. You may have spaces in a multifamily dwelling for only one or two cars per unit. If a tenant has more than that number of cars, you may want to charge extra for parking spots. Keep in mind that for a person with a disability, you may be required to provide parking access near his or her unit. It's a good idea to find out the number of cars a tenant will have and to get the license numbers as well.

Can you pay in cash all the money owed before you move in?

Often a tenant is required to pay first and last month's rent (whether on a lease or on a month-to-month tenancy) plus a hefty cleaning deposit. Frequently tenants cannot come up with all the cash at once and will ask if they can pay you a portion now and a portion within a few weeks, or after the first month. Savvy landlords will refuse this request. The whole purpose of getting a last month's rent and a cleaning/security deposit is to ensure the tenant's compliance with your rules, including keeping the place clean and making timely rent payments. If the tenant can't provide the cash up front, you won't have the financial security requirements you need.

13

Have You Lined Up Your Financing?

QUESTIONS TO ASK YOURSELF

Are investor mortgages available?

These days, everyone seems to be an expert on mortgages. The probable reason is that so many people have refinanced their homes and have been through the lending process that they feel confident about speaking on the subject. The problem is that when you're an investor, as opposed to someone who's buying a property to live in, different lending rules apply. Basically, loans to investors usually carry a slightly higher interest rate and a slightly lower *LTV* (*loan-to-value ratio*). Thus, while an owner/occupant can get a mortgage for 100 percent (or more) of the purchase price, most investors are lucky to get a mortgage for 90 percent. Further, these investor loans are often written with an interest rate that is half a percent or more higher and may include extra points.

Do I understand why lenders don't favor investors?

The reason is that lenders sometimes see investors as offering an additional risk. When hard times hit an owner/occupant, that person is likely to dig in and keep making the payments to save his or her homestake. When hard times hit an investor, it becomes a business decision: make the payments with the hope of coming out later on, or simply allow the property to go into foreclosure. Lenders worry that investors may find the second option too easy—hence, the perception of greater risk and thus, less attractive mortgages.

What if I'm an investor with lots of property?

Woe unto you! Investors who already have rental property may end up needing a higher personal income to qualify for a mortgage. The reason is that many lenders will not allow you to apply all of your rental income toward new financing. On the other hand, they will require you to note all of the expenses you have. That means that even if your property breaks even, you still need some extra income in order to balance out the expenses. That's why an investor with multiple properties often needs a higher income to qualify for the same mortgage as an investor with no additional properties.

Where do I get investor financing?

It's available from essentially the same places that everyone else gets financing. Check with a good mortgage broker or a bank. Simply state that you're an investor, and the lender will handle all of the paperwork.

Can I get an occupant's mortgage?

Probably, if you're going to be an owner/occupant. Many first-time investors will buy a home with the intent of living in it. Then, after a period of time typically lasting one to two years, they'll rent it out. They'll convert that home into a rental. The advantage of doing this is that as an owner/occupant you're eligible for some of the best financing in the world. Assuming that you can get a conforming loan (one currently under $359,600 that conforms to Fannie Mae or Freddie Mac underwriting standards), you may be able to get in for 5 percent down. In some cases, it can be nothing down. In rarer cases, the lender can arrange to increase the loan amount to 103 to 107 percent in order to cover your closing costs. Is it any wonder that new investors most frequently start out by buying a property in which to live?

Do I really have to move in?

Keep in mind that we're talking about actually moving into the home and living there—occupying it. The great temptation for investors is to say they will live in the property in order to get the good financing and then not actually move in, renting the place out instead. This is simply lying, and if you do it, it could land you in real hot water. Almost all mortgages are in some way insured, guaranteed, or resold through government or quasi-government agencies. That means that if you lie and are caught, you will have to do a lot of explaining to the Treasury Department. Penalties could be anything from a demand to repay the full amount of the loan immediately to indictment on criminal charges. All of which is to say if you're going to put down that you intend to occupy the property, be sure you in fact do that. Later on, after you've lived there for a while, you can think about converting it to a rental.

Will the seller finance my purchase?

One of the best ways for an investor to finance real estate is to have the seller carry some or all of the "paper." In effect, the seller gives the buyer a loan to help make the purchase. While this has become a rarity in most residential real estate, it's still fairly common practice in many areas of the country where commercial real estate and land is sold. Seller financing has many advantages:

- There's no trouble getting funding. The seller simply carries back the loan.
- Frequently it's easier qualifying. Many sellers, anxious to make a sale, will overlook some credit blemishes that an institutional lender might balk at.
- The interest rate is negotiable, depending on how eager the seller is to dispose of the property.
- There are no points. Most sellers simply don't think in the same terms that lenders do.

How do I arrange seller financing?

It's usually arranged at the time you make your purchase offer. You put into the purchase offer a contingency that the sale is subject to your obtaining a mortgage from the seller. Of course, you include the desired interest rate, term, and so forth. In other words, you make the deal contingent upon your obtaining seller financing. If the seller won't give it to you, there's no deal. Make the price good enough, and any seller will at least seriously consider the offer.

How do I get cash out?

Cashing out usually, but not always, occurs after you own the property. It means getting a mortgage that not only pays off your existing financing, but also cashes in some of your equity. In the past, this was the single most difficult problem for investors. Today it's easier. In many cases you can get an 80 percent mortgage, including cash back to you. In some cases, 90 percent is available with cash back on a refinancing. But you do have to search around. Again, you'll probably pay a stiffer interest rate and more points, and you will need more personal income to qualify. But at least the financing is there.

Can I get a second mortgage?

Generally speaking, the *combined loan-to-value* (*CLTV*) ratio for a second mortgage is the same as it would be for a large first mortgage: 80 to 90 percent. However, the higher interest rate and points usually apply only to the second mortgage, not the first. When this type of second mortgage is paired with a lower-interest-rate first mortgage, the combined interest rate sometimes can be lower than it would be for a single large new refinanced mortgage. There are also private investors who will give you cash out. However, they tend to charge much higher interest rates, and the loans tend to be for a much shorter term.

Can I get financing based on my other assets?

Yet another type of financing is to borrow not on the property you are buying, but on other property such as stocks or bonds that you already own. The advantage in securing this type of financing is that you can obtain loans at very low interest rates, often through stockbrokers and banks. Banks sometimes offer these loans to investors. Experienced real estate investors also frequently borrow on property they already own in order to make a new purchase. For example, you may have an apartment building that you bought several years ago and in which you have substantial equity. You refinance this property and use the funds to buy a new property. The assets you use can be almost anything. You need a creative banker or mortgage lender to handle this type of financing.

Can I get relatives to help out?

When they start out, many investors do. They go to their parents, brothers, sisters, or anyone else they feel they can tap for a loan. Ideally it would be a personal loan, but sometimes the relative will insist on having a mortgage on the property or an interest in it. You have to judge whether the money you're getting warrants the equity you're giving away. Another method is to share owner-ship. Typically you'll handle the management of the property, and when it's time to sell, the family will split up the profits. This system, of course, is not limited to families. It will work with friends or even perfect strangers. However, a word of caution: put everything in writing. People, even close relatives, often forget what was said months or years earlier. When it's time to sell, you want to have in writing exactly how the profits (or if something goes wrong, the losses) are to be split up. Fur-ther, you want to be sure that there are solid escape clauses allowing you, or another party, to exit the deal if situations change. (For example, you could lose your job, or your sibling, friend, son, or daughter could need to move out of the area.) And remember, relatives never for-get . . . and many never forgive if anything goes wrong.

CREDIT CARD FINANCING

Some more daring investors will make purchases using anything from cash withdrawals on a credit card to prom-issory notes. Contrary to most thinking, there's really nothing wrong with this, if it gets you into a good prop-erty and IF its short term. Why not borrow cash on a credit card if within a month or two you can secure per-manent long-term financing on the property and pay back the credit card loan (along with the horrendous inter-est charged)? The catch, of course, is to understand that this type of financing can only be very short term—a month or two. You must have a workable plan for paying it back quickly, else the interest charged will do you in. Sometimes this is a solution when you need to move very quickly—just days—on a bargain, and you can't wait to get a mortgage. The plan is to buy on short-term debt, then quickly refinance it out on a long-term mortgage. The danger, of course, is that you won't be able to get a mortgage, or not one of a high enough amount.

QUESTIONS TO ASK A LENDER

Can you get me investor financing?

Don't assume that all lenders are equal. Some specialize only in owner-occupied residential real estate. They may not know how to get investor financing. Others specialize in commercial real estate and are quite familiar with the type of financing you want. Be sure to look for a lender/mortgage broker who can adequately handle your needs. Be wary when the lender says something like, "We handle all kinds of financing." You don't want all kinds—you want a specific kind.

Can you tell me how big a mortgage I can get?

Preapproval in residential owner-occupied real estate is easy and commonly done. Investor pre approval is more complicated, particularly if some of your income/ expenses are attributable to other investment real estate you already own. The lender/mortgage broker must break down that other income to come up with a figure for how much it helps/hinders your ability to get new financing. A good lender will be able to tackle the job and quickly come up with an accurate answer. That's something you want and need if you're going to go out and buy more investment real estate.

QUESTIONS TO ASK A SELLER

Will you carry back paper?

While you might wonder why a seller would want to carry back a mortgage, rest assured, it's the sort of thing many sellers actually prefer to do. In the case of an older seller, he or she may intend using the equity taken from the house to live on in retirement. Getting that money out in cash may mean investing in low-interest-rate CDs. Keeping it in the form of a mortgage can mean double the interest—something such a seller may be very excited about. Of course, you'll need to convince the seller that you're reliable: not about to simply buy the property, rent it for a few months, and then walk off, leaving the seller to do a costly foreclosure. This is usually accomplished by sweetening the deal with a bigger down payment. Most sellers would prefer 20 percent down when carrying back a mortgage. Many will accept 10 percent. Few will be happy about doing the deal with anything less, regardless of the "no down payment" scenarios many so-called real estate gurus seem to promote.

How much equity do you have in the property?

In order for the seller to be able to offer you financing, he or she must either own the property free and clear or have substantial equity. A seller who has no equity can't finance you, the buyer. Therefore, you need to determine just what the seller has to play with. Although this question is asked less frequently today in an era of mostly institutional financing, it is still appropriate. You can begin by asking if the seller will carry back a mortgage. If the seller is agreeable, then your next question should be directed toward just how much, which is really asking about equity.

What terms will you accept?

It's important to remember that seller financing is entirely negotiable. The interest rate, length of the mortgage, whether it's amortized (paid in equal payments) or has no payments and just a balloon at the end is up to you and the seller. Find out what the seller hopes to accomplish with the mortgage, and then try to get the best terms.

14

Flip versus Serial Investing?

QUESTIONS TO ASK YOURSELF

Am I in for the long haul?

Whether you're interested in flipping properties or serial investing is usually determined by your long-term goals. If you're a person who expects to continue investing in real estate for 10, 20, or 30 years, then you can *serial invest*. This means buying a property and renting it out, buying a second and renting it out, then a third, and so on, acquiring wealth over time. On the other hand, if you're in for the short term, then you're probably looking mainly for properties that you can flip—quickly buy and resell. Since these tend to be few and far between, chances are you won't be doing much buying and selling. But when you do, you may walk away with tens of thousands of dollars or more in profit. Decide what your timeline is before you get started, and you won't end up disappointed with your real estate experience. But remember, the most successful investors are those in it for the long haul. (And there's nothing to keep a serial investor from flipping a property when the opportunity arises.)

Do I really understand flipping?

Flipping has always been around in real estate. But the term became popular during the last decade with the huge run up in real estate prices in many parts of the country. Savvy investors began to see that they could quickly gain control of a property and then resell for a profit. They didn't need to hold onto it for a long time. Indeed, they didn't even need to take title in some cases.

Thus, flipping means a quick buy and sell. It's the fastest way to make profits in real estate. And in some respects, the most dangerous. In order to flip you need to be able to carry out the following three actions:

1. Find a property below market price.
2. Gain control of that property.
3. Quickly resell.

Do I understand the dangers of flipping?

Flipping is fraught with risk. There are the risks of not being able to resell quickly. There are all the risks of getting angry sellers who feel they have been gypped. After all, you're buying low and selling high. The sellers may feel that the profits rightly should be theirs, not yours. Whether using an option or an assignment (described below), you should seek the advice of a good real estate attorney when flipping.

What are my transaction costs?

The bane of short-term real estate investors is the transaction costs. A round-trip (buying and then selling) is typically 10 percent of the sales price. That includes the title insurance and escrow charges on both ends, as well as any points and lender's fees when buying and a real estate commission when selling. This means, therefore, that in order to buy, flip, and make a profit, you must be able to sell for more than the typical 10 percent in transaction costs. If you flip a property for 20 percent, you've made 10 percent. If you flip it for 5 percent, you've lost 5 percent. Of course, many investors seek to reduce transaction costs by selling without an agent. However, that can take time and doesn't always produce results.

Can I avoid transaction costs when flipping?

Some savvy investors avoid all of the transaction costs by never actually completing the purchase when flipping. They, in effect, sell the property in escrow. The profit comes from gaining control at a fixed low price, and then selling to a "rebuyer" at a higher price. The rebuyer and the original seller pay all of the normal closing costs. The flipper walks away with the profit. Note: The action of an investor who buys a property and holds it for, say, six months and then resells at a profit is also generically called flipping. However, here it's more a matter of having bought well and riding up fast appreciation in the marketplace.

Should I do an "option flip"?

The simplest way to flip property without actually taking ownership, and thus avoiding transaction costs, is the real estate option. Real estate options are similar to stock options. For the buyer, you have the opportunity (but not the requirement) to purchase for a set price by some future date. For the seller, you are committed to sell, usually for a set price by a set date. You, the investor, locate the property and make an option offer. If the sellers accept, you next give them option money (perhaps $1,000) and they in exchange give you the right to purchase the property as noted above, usually at a fixed price, for up to a certain amount of time, typically no more than six months or a year. Next, you find a rebuyer, someone who will purchase the property from you at a higher price. Finally, you exercise the option at the low fixed price agreed upon by the seller, and then sell to the rebuyer at the new higher price, keeping the difference, which is the profit. In actual practice, all of these moves are made simultaneously and are handled in escrow, and the seller pays the normal seller's closing costs and the rebuyer pays the normal buyer's closing costs with very few transaction costs left for you to pay. The difference is what you pocket. In an option, you the buyer are not committed to purchase. It's at your discretion. The seller, however, is committed to sell, usually at a fixed price. He or she must go through with the transaction if you execute your option.

Do I have to pay taxes on the option profit?

Any time you make a profit, you're going to be liable for taxes. With an option, the taxes usually must be taken as ordinary income, since you may not qualify for the one-year wait for long-term capital gain. Check with a good accountant as there are fine points and tricks to the tax situation here.

Do I understand the time problem with options?

Time is the biggest problem with flipping using an option. Typically, options run to six months, although they can be for virtually any length of time. The trouble is that sellers usually want out quickly, and a seller who is willing to give you an option of more than 60 days is unlikely to be willing to also give you a good price. On the other hand, if you accept a shorter-term option, you put yourself in a more dangerous position. What happens if you can't find a rebuyer within, for example, 30 days? You lose your option money—and any potential deal.

Do I need a "rebuyer"?

Keep in mind that the key to a successful option flip is to have a rebuyer waiting and ready to go. If you have that rebuyer ready, you can handle a transaction easily in 60 days. Indeed, you might handle it in 30 days, or perhaps even less. But if you have to go out and find a rebuyer once you have the option, time puts a stranglehold on your potential success in the deal.

Should I do an "assignment flip"?

An assignment of purchase is yet another way to handle a flip. In this type of arrangement, you make an offer to purchase, usually for cash. However, when you make your offer, you state that the buyer is either your name *or assigns*. What this means is that either you can buy the property yourself, or you can assign the contract to someone else who will then buy the property. Later on, you have your rebuyer step in and you assign the purchase contract to him or her. Your rebuyer actually gets the financing and makes the purchase. And you pocket the difference between what you paid for the property and a higher price that the rebuyer pays. Getting a seller to agree to an assignment, however, can be tricky. Some sellers won't go along with an assignment sales contract. The reason is that they don't know who will eventually purchase the property. They are afraid that you might not be able to get a needed mortgage and want a backdoor out, or that you're planning to sell your contract to someone else (which is, in fact, the case!) and that person may not qualify for a needed mortgage. In order to calm the seller's fears, you may need to put up a bigger deposit or avoid putting many escape clauses into the contract, which can increase your risks.

How quickly can I do an assignment?

The ability to assign the contract runs only as long as the purchase contract is in effect, typically 30 to 45 days. That means that you've got to find a buyer and conclude the other end of the deal very quickly. It can work if your rebuyer is ready and waiting. The rebuyer picks up the assignment and moves forward with the purchase of the property. Again, you never actually make the purchase. The transaction is basically handled in escrow. At the end of the deal, you get your money out, typically in cash.

Do I actually have to buy the property in an assignment?

You might have to if you don't have a rebuyer. Remember, you're signing a purchase agreement that's intended to be legally binding. If you (or the assignee) fail to go through with the purchase, the deposit is at risk. Further, an angry seller might even sue for specific performance, asking for damages because you failed to complete the transaction.

Can I protect myself?

You'll want to include "escape clauses." These are contingencies that you insert into the contract that let you out. A typical contingency is financing: don't get the mortgage, you're not committed to buy. Savvy flippers often have a whole list of contingencies they insert to provide escape avenues for them. However, keep in mind that escape clauses weaken your offer and lessen your chances of getting it accepted. So to make the deal, you may not be able to include many (or any) and may have to take a big risk.

Should I disclose my profits?

This is one way of helping to be sure that neither the rebuyer nor the seller can claim that you pulled a fast one.

Be perfectly on the up and up and tell everyone exactly the nature of the deal you're making and how much profit you're realizing. And get it in writing in case one of the parties later has a failure of memory. If all the parties know exactly what's happening and still go forward, there's not much to complain about later. Of course, some flippers wonder if they can make the big profit if the seller knows what's happening. My take on that is: if a deal can't withstand the scrutiny of all parties knowing what's going on, then it's probably an inherently bad deal. And you're probably better off not getting involved in it.

Am I aware of the publicity regarding bad flips?

It's important to remember that you don't operate in a vacuum. Other people have been flipping properties for years and their successes—or failures— can haunt you. In recent years, a few investors working with a few unscrupulous appraisers bought property not at discount, but at full price. Then the appraisers came in with very high appraisals. The properties were then sold at above-market prices using nothing-down financing— often to ethnic minorities or immigrants who did not speak English well. Later, these rebuyers discovered they could not make the high mortgage payments and lost the properties to foreclosure. The federal government, as the ultimate guarantor of much of the country's real estate financing, ended up taking them back. When it discovered what was going on, it turned the matter over to the Treasury Department and the FBI, which have been working to uncover the perpetrators of this scam. For you as an honest investor, the problem is that many sellers are now biased against flips because they've read about what dishonest people have done. It only makes your job harder.

Can I flip brand new properties?

Sometimes. When prices are accelerating by double digits, it's a real temptation to try to lock in a new property and then quickly flip it. It usually works like this. Builders like to presell their homes. They take deposits on properties that are not going to be built for six months or more. So, the savvy investor puts down a $500 deposit and waits. Six months later prices may have gone up by 10 percent. So the investor then sells his or her rights to purchase to a rebuyer and pockets the 10 percent of the sales price in cash, as a profit. It's a nifty deal. The problem is, today's builders will rarely accept a contract that includes an assignment. Rather, they want whoever puts up the original deposit to actually complete the purchase. (Some builders have even tried to insert clauses into their sales contract prohibiting flipping.) If you can't complete it, they often will be happy to refund your deposit since, after all, they can now sell to the next buyer for 10 percent more themselves. And if you go through with the transaction and try to resell, remember the transaction costs. Those could eat up any profit you have. Nevertheless, savvy investors have flipped new properties. They have gotten builders to go along with assignments by claiming hardships, that the rebuyers were relatives, and on and on. All of which is to say that you might be able to flip a new property. And then again, you might not.

Do I really understand serial investing?

The premise behind serial investing is quite simple. You buy properties, usually single-family homes, one at a time. You buy them regularly, perhaps one every year or one every two years. You rent these properties and you don't sell them, unless you need the money or there's an opportunity to flip and make a big profit. Over time, you acquire many good properties, and after 15 or 20 years you may have dozens or more of them. The tenants slowly pay down the mortgages as your equity rises. As you need cash, you can refinance or sell them. After two decades of serial investing, your net worth can easily exceed several million dollars. And you've made all of this money with relatively little risk and in your spare time. Is it any wonder that so many people have become serial real estate investors?

Do I know the drawbacks of serial real estate investing?

The drawbacks are the same as for any real estate investment. Unlike dealing with stocks and bonds, property is not liquid. In an emergency you may not be able to liquidate quickly and get your money out. Also, if there is an economic decline, or you bought in a poor location, or you simply have bad luck, you could find it difficult to keep the properties fully rented, in which case you'd have trouble making your mortgage payments, taxes, and other expenses. Finally, although it's been going up virtually every year since the Great Depression when they started keeping accurate records, there's nothing to say that real estate won't decline at some point in the future.

Can I take advantage of the financing benefits?

One of the big advantages of serial investing comes about if you're willing to live in the property you're buying. Owner/occupant mortgages offer the best financing in the world. You may be able to get in for almost no money down, yet get the lowest possible interest rate. Here's how it works. You buy the property not as an investment, but as your home. You move and live in the home for a year or two (or as long as your tax accountant tells you it's appropriate). Then you move out and convert the property to a rental. You, hopefully, rent it for all of your expenses, including taxes, insurance, mortgage payments, and maintenance and repairs. Finally, you go out and find another house to buy and in which to live. You keep repeating the process. Notice that instead of selling one house to buy the next, you keep each house. After several decades, you've acquired as many as a dozen properties or more. And, in each of these, tenants are paying the expenses for you. It all comes about because of the wonderful financing offered to owner/occupants. Note that there could be potential problems. For one, some mortgages explicitly prohibit renting out a property bought as an owner/occupant. Legal experts, however, are mixed about whether such a clause is enforceable. I've never seen a lender attempt to enforce it.

How long must I live in the property before converting?

This is a gray area and one about which you should consult with your tax professional. Some experts say that living in the home for two years before you convert it to a rental should be okay. Others say only a year. And some risk-taking buyers only live in it a month or two. But be careful about not moving in at all. You might argue that your *intent* was to move in, but your circumstances changed and you were forced to convert the property to a rental. You might get away with it once. But if you did it 10 times in a row, it would be pretty evident that you never intended to move in. And lenders and their federal government overseers can get quite angry at and take legal action against people who blatantly use owner/occupant financing for outright purchases of investment property.

Can I convert back?

Some investors will convert a home to a rental and keep it as such for many, many years. However, before they sell, they then convert it back to a personal residence in order to claim the up to $500,000 capital gains exclusion available to married couples filing jointly. (See also Chapter 18.) The rule is you must have lived in the property for two out of the previous five years in order to claim the exclusion. If you've previously done a Section 1031 tax-deferred exchange, you must have lived in the property for five out of the previous five years. (Check with your accountant.)

Can I do a tax deferred exchange?

This is available only on investment property. It, in effect, lets you trade one piece of investment/business property for a "like-kind" other. If the trade is structured properly, there's no immediate tax to pay. Instead, it is all deferred. However, such exchanges can be tricky. Check with your accountant, and also see Chapter 18.

15

Where Are the Profits in Foreclosures?

QUESTIONS TO ASK YOURSELF

Do I understand foreclosures?

Foreclosure is the process whereby lenders take back properties from borrowers almost always because of failure to repay. These properties can be run-down shacks in the worst corner of town, or they can be mansions in the best neighborhoods. In an average year, there are well over 400,000 foreclosures nationwide with more than a million owners who are between 30 and 90 days overdue on their loan payments—and possibly on their way to foreclosure. Of course, when the real estate market dips, foreclosures increase. It's been estimated that because of the large amount of nothing-down, interest-only adjustable-rate financing in recent years, foreclosure rates could skyrocket during the next real estate recession. Foreclosures can provide a strong investing opportunity *if* they can be purchased below market. Since not all foreclosed property is a good deal (as when an owner is upside down, or owes more than the property is worth), an investor has to be very careful when moving into this field. On the other hand, sometimes properties in foreclosure can be had for pennies on the dollar.

Do I know the three times during the foreclosure process that I can buy a foreclosure?

The foreclosure process is not standardized across the country. Instead, it varies from state to state. A lot depends on whether your state uses a trust deed (which can be foreclosed privately) or a mortgage (which must use a judicial foreclosure). Generally speaking, however, there are three times during the foreclosure process when an investor can step in and purchase the property:

1. When the borrower hasn't made the payments and the lender has declared the mortgage is in default. You have to buy the property directly from the borrower and correct the default, usually by refinancing.

2. When the trustee or the court sells the property "on the courthouse steps." The lender is there to bid the full amount of the defaulted loan plus back interest and costs. You can bid higher.

3. When the lender now owns the property (called an REO). You must buy directly from the lender since the original borrower is usually out of the picture.

Am I aware of the dangers of buying a foreclosure?

When you purchase a home not in foreclosure, typically everything is out in the open for you. You know who the seller actually is. You know what the existing financing on the property may be. You know what rights to the property the seller may retain, even after the sale. With a foreclosure, much of that vital information is hidden from you. You must dig it out yourself. Here are some of the pitfalls when dealing with foreclosures:

1. No one may want to deal with you. The seller may be angry and, even though anxious to sell for financial reasons, may really want to keep the property for emotional reasons. Thus, every step forward toward a purchase also can become a step backward.

2. Similarly, the existing lender may not want to talk with you because you have no standing with the mortgage. Thus, you may have trouble determining if the financing you see is really a first, a second, or some even more junior mortgage. Unless you know all of the financing on the property, you can't truly determine the owner's equity . . . and how to pay for it.

3. It can be difficult to get title insurance. You may need to wait until after the purchase to get title insurance. And then it could be too late to protect yourself.

4. The current owner/seller may have a right of redemp-
    tion. In some states, when there is a foreclosure, even a
    judicial foreclosure, the previous owner may be able to
    come back and regain title to the property by paying
    off all back liens and debts. That could be an obstacle
    to your getting new financing or even reselling.

Do I know the special perils of buying "default" foreclosures?

Many investors are tempted to buy a property directly
from the borrower when it is first in default, or on the
courthouse steps when it is publicly sold. Indeed, it is at
these two times that you are most likely to get the lowest
price. Unfortunately, it is also at these times that you're
most likely to make a big money mistake. There are several
reasons, but one of the biggest is that in the early stages
you may not know just what you're getting. While you
may think you're bidding on a *first mortgage*, you may actually be bidding on a second, or even a third. The order of
mortgages determines the order in which lenders are paid.
(Firsts get paid first, only then, if there's money left, does a
second get paid, then a third, and so forth.) If you get a secondary mortgage, while you may believe you're getting a
bargain, a higher mortgage may actually be on the property and may amount to all of your profit and more.

Do I understand "buyer's redemption" rights?

The second problem is that when dealing directly with
sellers in default, you may not get clear title. Indeed,
defaulting sellers in many states often have a long period
of *redemption*. This means that even after you think you've
gotten title, they may have the right to come back and
claim the property (after paying off the debt). Thus,
investors seeking to buy property directly from borrowers or at a foreclosure sale are advised to get the aid of an
experienced professional. At least when you first get
started, it is mandatory to have the advice of an attorney
and an agent familiar with foreclosures.

Where can I learn about properties in foreclosure?

As soon as a lender files a notice of default, it becomes public knowledge. (A default notice lets the borrower officially

know that he or she is in arrears and that the foreclosure process has begun.) These are published in a local legal paper. Find the legal paper and check it out. One problem with this, however, is that often the location of the property is given as a legal description, such as a lot and tract number recorded in a certain county map. Street addresses are seldom given. Hence, you'll need to go to the recorder's office and look up the description, which will lead you to a map on which streets and addresses can be interpreted. Another alternative is to take the legal description to a title insurance company where for a fee (or free if you're familiar with one of the officers) it can be translated. Alternatively, many areas offer foreclosure newsletters. Published here is not only the common street address, but sometimes the phone number of the borrower/seller and that of the lender. Another alternative is to make friends with an officer in a title company. Since these are the people who normally handle trust deed foreclosures, they are in a position to give you advance knowledge of the filing of notices of default. Finally, there's the Internet, where a host of sites (such as www.foreclosure.com or www.foreclosuresnet. net) offer information. However, keep in mind that they are usually national sites and the foreclosure you're looking at may actually be in another state.

Do I understand the advantages of REOs?

REO stands for *real estate owned*. After a property has been sold on the courthouse steps to the lender (typically the highest bidder), it moves from the asset side of the ledger (where it was a performing loan), to the debit side where it's listed as a liability—a property owned by the lender. The reason it's considered a liability is that the lender, presumably, is not in the business of owning real estate, but instead in the business of making mortgages. Taking back property through foreclosure represents a failure on the lender's part. Too many such failures and a federal regulatory agency may step in and declare the lender insolvent. Hence, lenders are most anxious to get rid of their REOs.

Why don't lenders promote sales of REOs?

They do, but quietly. Lenders desperately want to get rid of these properties, but they don't want it widely known that they have them. If the public knows the lender has a lot of foreclosures, it may begin withdrawing deposits, thus forcing the lender closer to insolvency. Hence, most lenders today fix up the REOs they take back (typically they're in terrible shape after a borrower, angered over being foreclosed, has trashed the property), and list them with real estate agents. They are on the market along with all the other properties, and are competitively priced. They just aren't advertised as REOs.

Do I understand the opportunities in REOs?

Buying a REO through an agent on the open market is no different from buying any other property. It's in competition with all the rest on the MLS (multiple listing service). However, if you can get to the lender *before* it lists the property—indeed, even before it fixes it up—you might be able to get a terrific deal. This is particularly the case when the real estate market goes sour and lenders have lots of REOs. If an investor comes in and offers to buy one or more of them, "as is," (without warranties or fix up), lenders are often tempted. A quick sale and disposal, even at a loss, can be better than keeping REOs on the books for a long period of time. I've bought REOs directly from lenders in this condition, often for a fraction of their value. Of course, then it's up to the buyer to get the property back into shape and rent it out or flip it.

Do I know the problems with REOs?

Often these are cash deals. Most lenders prefer all cash for them. That way they get rid of the property once and for all. That means that you may have to secure the financing through other lenders. (A few REO lenders do recognize the fact that they will get less from a cash offer, so agree to handle the financing themselves for a higher sales price. Sometimes they'll even throw in a cash credit toward having the property fixed up.) In addition, there could be the following problems when buying a REO:

1. *Sold "As Is."* The lender/seller often makes no warranty to you of any kind. This means that if you discover a problem after the sale, it's your headache, not the lender's. (That's why the price is cheaper!)

2. *Few Disclosures.*   While most states now require sellers to provide disclosure statements, this may not
   apply to a lender who is federally chartered. The lender
   may refuse to give you any kind of disclosure statement. Or, if you do get disclosures, they may disclose
   virtually nothing, the lender claiming it knows nothing
   about the property. Once again, you're on your own.

3. *No Repairs.*   Some lenders will fix up the property,
   but then charge full price. On the other hand, to get a
   lower price you may need to buy the property in the
   same condition as left by the previous owner. You'll
   want the most thorough inspector you can find. However, don't expect the lender to do anything toward
   correcting problems the inspector finds. Typically,
   beyond basic refurbishing, most lenders will make no
   repairs of any kind, even if the inspector finds problems that are a safety issue. (In that case, the lender
   may insist you sign a statement that you accept the
   property at your own risk!)

How do I get lenders to offer me "raw" REOs?

Find out who the biggest real estate lenders are in your
community. Become a depositor, even a borrower. Find
out who handles their REOs. (The REO officer is rarely
listed as such by the lender.) Make friends. A business
lunch would not be out of order. Explain that you're an
investor looking to make an honest profit. If you can help
out the lender by taking an REO off its hands in a quick,
cash deal, you'd be happy to do it. It's a case where con-
tacts can pay off.

Do I have to pay cash for a REO?

Not necessarily. If it's a good property, the lender may be
willing to offer financing (typically with your putting at
least 10 percent down). In some cases, the lender may
even offer a cleaning/fix-up allowance. In most cases,
however, the lender just wants the property off its hands.
That means that you'll need to secure financing elsewhere. Keep in mind that there is no end of lenders who
will be happy to work with you on financing another
lender's REO. If you set up outside financing in advance

(something not hard to do), you can come to the lender who has the REO and offer it a cash deal. That has proven irresistible to many lenders in the past, and should continue to do so.

Should I try tax sales?

Tax sales offer a variety of opportunities to ambitious real estate investors. These involve properties on which the owner has not paid taxes. Hence, the state takes them back. In some cases, there are actual auctions at which you can bid on the properties. In most cases, however, there are tax lien sales in which you essentially pay the debt owed to the state by the property owner and you get a tax lien on the property. This lien usually carries a handsome interest rate and you're assured that either the owner will eventually pay it off, in order to save the property, or the property will go to auction, in which case either you'll get it or get your note paid back. These sales are conducted all across the country in most states, which means that, if you're interested, you're going to be doing quite a bit of traveling. You can find out about them by contacting local tax officials. Some Internet sites also promote them. However, be aware that this is not a gift of money to you. You must investigate the properties to be sure they are worth at least as much, if not more, than the taxes owed. And there are other factors, such as competitive bidding, to be wary of. A number of books have recently come out on this subject including *Profit by Investing in Real Estate Tax Liens* by Larry Loftis (Dearborn, 2004). You should also check with a good attorney in the state in which you're going to be working to be sure you're complying with all the rules and regulations regarding tax sales.

Should I bid on probate properties?

A number of years ago, properties were frequently in probate. Today, however, many owners put their real estate in a revocable trust and it passes to their heirs without ever going up for auction. Nonetheless, people still do die without trusts, and their real estate is sold through probate, which is essentially a legal process for disposing of a deceased person's property as well as for the paying of his or her creditors. Probate sales may or may not be open for public bidding. Sometimes an executor or administrator of an estate will ask some friends in real estate if they want to purchase a property out of probate. A sale might be obtained in this fashion, and if a judge goes along, the deal is done. More frequently, however, in order to secure the best price, the property will be open for public bidding. Typically this is done in two parts. In the first part, the administrator/executor accepts sealed bids. In the second part, the sealed bids are opened in a courtroom and then the judge asks if there's anyone else who wants to bid. At this point, public bidding may occur. Sometimes probate properties can be bought for a fraction of their cost. If, however, the sale is well publicized, there may be many bidders and the price can be bid up well beyond the property's actual value. I've bid on probate properties and I can tell you it's a tricky business. I suggest you have a good professional, such as an agent or attorney experienced in this field, advise you before you attempt it.

16
Ready to Try Office and Commercial Buildings?

QUESTIONS TO ASK YOURSELF

Am I ready to move into commercial real estate?

Many real estate investors spend their entire careers at the single-family home level and do very well at it. But for those who hunger for bigger deals, the answer is usually larger properties. The plusses include positive cash flow (sometimes from the moment of purchase), professional management (which becomes more affordable when dealing with multiple units), and sometimes very large profits when you sell. It's not hard to imagine why investors want to move up to larger properties. But, along with the plusses are some minuses. You will generally have more of your own money at risk; the lease structures can be complicated, even arcane; and if there's a recession or a problem with the property, you can have massive vacancies. My suggestion is that you start out simple, in single-family homes. Once you have a taste for it, you can spread out into other areas of real estate. Some investors, in fact, make the transition very quickly . . . and successfully.

Do I understand the new dynamics?

With single-family homes, profits usually come when you sell. Until then, you typically hang on hoping to achieve positive cash flow, but often having to accept some negative cash flow. Prices are largely determined not by how much you can rent the property for, but by how much similar homes sell for. With larger buildings, it's a somewhat different story. While negative cash flow can sometimes be a problem, prices are tied directly to income. The higher the rents, the higher the value of the property. Notice the difference. With single-family homes, profits come when a neighborhood of mostly owner/occupant owners goes up in value. In larger buildings, profits go up when you're able to raise rents. In single-family homes, you're tied to the sales market. In larger buildings, you're tied to the rental market.

Do I understand the relationship between rents and price?

The simplest way of evaluating an office or commercial building is to use the GIM (gross income multiplier, which was discussed in detail in Chapter 7). You find out what the gross annual rents are, and then multiply them by this number, which is actually derived from comparisons of similar buildings that have recently sold. What is important to understand is that if you double the rents, you double the value of the building. (In single-family homes, how much you receive in rent is virtually irrelevant when calculating price.) Thus, everything comes down to how much you can rent the property for. Many savvy investors spend entire days looking at apartment, office, and commercial buildings trying to find those where, for whatever reason, the current landlord/owner has not raised rents to market levels. They then try to buy those buildings based on the current low rents. Once they own the property, they do what's necessary to raise rents. This may involve fixing up the property, or getting newer and better tenants, or . . . ? In the end, the higher they are able to raise the rents, the more valuable the property becomes, and the more they are eventually able to sell it for.

Do I understand leases?

Although the dynamics of all commercial property are more or less as described above, leases also play a big role. The strength of the tenant leases also helps determine the property's value. Long-term leases with strong tenants (those likely to continue to pay their rents year after year with escalation clauses) mean a higher value.

Short-term leases and weak tenants mean a lower value. Improve the leases and you'll also improve the value. Of course, there are other factors. In commercial buildings, the value of the property generally declines as the height goes up. For example, a commercial tenant on a second-floor mall generally pays less than a tenant on the street level of that same mall. The reason is that there's normally less foot traffic on the second floor—it's not as good a location. The reverse is often true for office buildings, where the higher levels are considered more prestigious (until there's an earthquake or a disaster like 9/11).

Should I start with a small apartment building?

It's not a bad idea. My suggestion is that you look for something with around six to eight units. This means you'll still handle management and maintenance/repairs yourself. But, if you've already bought and sold single-family dwellings, you should be an old hand at this. Further, in this case all of the work is at one single location. You don't have to travel to lots of different spots to take care of your property.

Do I know how I will get financing?

Sometimes it's a problem. The banks may complain that you have no previous experience with apartment buildings (or commercial, or industrial, or whatever else you're starting out on). Further, you may already be stretched thin because of your other real estate holdings. As a result, instead of the high LTV (loan-to-value) ratios that you may have found common in single-family homes, you may discover that lenders won't give more than 70 to 80 percent loans. But, don't despair. Sellers are well aware of these problems and are much more likely to carry back paper (second mortgages). Unless you're very clever, however, you may find that you will indeed be required to come up with some cash.

Can I buy for nothing down?

Yes, it's done all the time. Investors get, for example, a 70 percent institutional loan. Then they get the sellers to carry back a 20 percent second. Then they borrow on other real estate they already own and get the remaining 10 percent. Voilà, they're into the commercial property with nothing down. However, beware of this technique. The big problem is making the payments on all that financing. Will the property's income cover it? Many investors are counting on raising rents in order to make their new hefty payments. If for some reason they are unable to do so, it could mean they would lose the property to foreclosure, and lose their good names and credit as well. Be very wary of commercial deals that don't involve any cash. Yes, they can be wonderful if everything works as planned. Or they can be disasters if things you're counting on go awry.

Have I verified the tenants?

When buying commercial and office buildings, but even more importantly apartment buildings, it's very important to verify who the tenants are and how much they are actually paying. It's not uncommon for prospective buyers to ask to see actual check-receipts from tenants and bank deposits from the seller. This helps to avoid nasty surprises later on. Don't be fooled into thinking that sellers are always on the up and up. It's happened more than once that an overeager seller has filled up the units with relatives paying no rent, or with others who are paying a discounted rent. An unsuspecting buyer purchases the property and suddenly discovers the scam. Now he or she has a big rent-up (and sometimes rent collection) problem. By the way, going after the seller can prove elusive and, even if successful, could take years.

Should I get into small commercial buildings?

Another natural starting place for investors looking to move up is commercial buildings. But, before you make an offer on Trump Towers, you might want to consider that strip mall down the street. Small neighborhood malls dot the landscape of our country and many are extremely profitable. Don't be put off by the fact that there are only a half dozen stores in them. The right tenants with good leases can turn the strip mall into a gold mine. Even better, the wrong tenants with bad leases on someone else's property can offer a diamond mine for the investor smart enough to see the problem, buy the property on the cheap, and get better tenants and leases. The key, of course, is finding it.

Should I work with agents?

Yes, of course. It makes no sense to reinvent the wheel, and agents are out there aplenty. Just be sure you get the right agent. Probably 95 percent of all agents work the residential market. They sell houses day in and day out. If you come to one of them asking about a strip mall, they might agree to show you some. Then, they'll quickly thumb through the MLS for commercial property and the next day you'll zoom out to see what's on the market. That could work. But far better would be for you to find an agent who specializes in commercial property. Sometimes, there's one agent in a large office that does so. Other times, whole offices are dedicated to commercial real estate. That's the kind you want to contact. However, just remember that you're going to be the new kid on the block, so don't try pushing your weight around too much. Ask, don't demand of commercial agents. They want to make a sale as much as you want a purchase and they'll be happy to work on a small deal, when time and energy permit.

Should I consider office buildings?

Yes, but probably not as a first venture. Office buildings can be very tricky and a lot depends on the office space market at the time. Residential and even commercial real estate can be booming and, at the same time, office space can be in a huge surplus with many vacancies. Office building vacancy rates can be astonishingly high when compared to residential property, sometimes reaching 25 percent or more. (I can remember being astonished to learn when visiting New York City a few years ago that some of the office space—at that time in the Empire State building—had never, ever been rented up! There just wasn't enough demand for it.) It's not just the economy, either. Many times it's simply supply and demand. Builders in the midst of an economic boom will often churn out office buildings. However, there is soon so much office space available that the square-foot costs plummet and much of it remains vacant. In some markets, it can take 10 or 12 years for demand to catch up with supply—longer if a recession intervenes. All of which is to say, if you're savvy about office space, then by all means jump in. But if you're wet behind the ears, I would look elsewhere. You just might hit the market during a down part of the cycle.

17

Should You Get Started in Bare Land?

QUESTIONS TO ASK YOURSELF

Do I understand what bare land investing involves?

☐

Those who invest in bare land go by various names. Those who buy bare land, build on it, and then sell are called *developers*. And those who buy broken-down buildings, scrape them off the land, and then build new structures are often *fixer-upper specialists*. And those who buy bare land and then resell it for a profit without developing it are often called *speculators*. This also tells us the basics of what can be done with bare land.

Is it hard to buy?

☐

In some ways, it's the hardest real estate investment to make and, in other ways, it's the easiest. The basic problem is in financing. While there's a whole system in place to handle mortgages on homes and even commercial property, nothing like that exists for bare land. Rather, about the only place you can get an institutional mortgage on such property is from a bank. And even then, the maximum LTV is often only 50 to 60 percent. That means that you as an investor must in some way handle 40 to 50 percent of the sales price—an impossible burden for most investors. That's the bad news. The good news is that most sellers of bare land are well aware of the problems involved in disposing of their property and are more than willing to help out. Often, they will finance the entire sale. Other times, they'll take back a second mortgage for a large part of the down payment. They're not altruistic.

They realize that this may be the only way to sell such property. And besides, they probably bought it for cash years ago and most of the sales price is going to be profit for them.

Where do I find bare land?

It could be anywhere, from out in the woods to the inner city. Bare land simply means land that hasn't been built on, yet. It's waiting for someone to purchase and develop it. That could be you. Or you could be a speculator, buying the land in the hopes of holding it for a time until it appreciates in value and then reselling. Remember, the building doesn't normally appreciate in value—rather, it depreciates over time. That's why the government allows investors to take depreciation as a tax write-off. The land, however, is what goes up (or down) in value as the market changes. When a home jumps in price from $200,000 to $500,000, it's not because the house itself went up (unless there were additions and renovations). It's because the land beneath it became more valuable.

Do I know the pros and cons of bare land investing?

The pros include:

- Sellers will often finance the deal.
- You don't have to worry about tenants or collecting rent.
- Profits can be very large.

The cons include:

- The turnover time is slow, unless there's a very hot market.
- Sometimes lots of cash is required.
- Bare land can be difficult to finance.

Should I look for "leftover" lots?

Leftover lots (sometimes called marginal lots) are typically located in urban and suburban settings. When a developer comes through and puts up housing or commercial buildings, sometimes a lot here and there will fall through the cracks. It never gets developed and sits there, often covered with weeds. Eventually, times change and the market becomes hot in the area. People are looking for homes. And that marginal lot suddenly becomes highly desirable. Usually, however, there are problems. Typically this lot is owned by a corporation or by someone who's had it in the family for years. It sits there waiting for the miracle buyer to come to buy it and pay a fortune for it. You can see its potential, but not if it costs a fortune. So your challenge is to find the owner and get him or her (or it) to sell it to you at a reasonable price. Look around in almost any area. You'll find lots that fit this description.

Are there special costs in developing "leftover" lots?

There may be. The lot could be too small, according to the planning department of the city, to build up. That would mean getting a variance from planning, something that might be hard and costly to do. (And that could be the reason it was initially never developed.) The lot may not have utilities to it, necessitating dragging them from a distance and at considerable expense. If utilities are there, it could cost a hefty sum to get them connected. And to develop the lot might mean costly building permits as well as donations of large sums of money toward schools.

Is the lot "developable"?

Does the lot have adequate egress and ingress, meaning you can get into and out of it? Are there any utilities available at any cost? Is the land itself buildable? Or are there obstacles too difficult to overcome, such as severe drainage issues or an earthquake fault underneath? Whenever you see an undeveloped lot among other developed lots—a leftover piece—be wary. There could be very good reasons it was never developed.

Should I consider a "scraper"?

This has become quite profitable in urban areas. Typically it's done by a contractor. However, anyone with a sense of adventure can tackle it. You find a good lot with a bad house on it. Usually the house is old and run down. Then you tear down the house or "scrape" it off the lot. Next, you erect a modern home, often far larger than the original. Finally, you sell the new home for a big profit. Generally speaking, with the rising costs of construction, this tends to work best in expensive neighborhoods where the cost of the house is a sizeable portion of the overall value of the property. Also, there are a few tricks to the process. One is to see if you can use the utility hookups of the old house, thus avoiding the payment of a connection charge. In other cases, you might avoid being assessed on the entire lot and house if a portion of the old home is saved—you turn it into a remodel instead of a complete scraper. Finally, as with fixer-uppers (Chapter 11), you must buy the property with the old house on it cheaply enough to make the entire process affordable.

Can I do a land split?

A land split can be one of the easiest or one of the most difficult methods of generating money. Basically, you buy a lot and then split it into two, three, or more parcels. The sum of the value of the parcels, hopefully, is more than the value of the single large lot. The most common split I've seen is when someone has a large lot and then builds a house on one portion of it. An investor buys the property and, presuming zoning laws allow, divides it into two separate lots, selling off the excess land as a bare lot. Sometimes you can reap enough money from the lot to pay for the entire previous purchase of the house with the excess land! (A mortgage covering the entire property may prevent splitting.)

Should I try an agricultural land split?

Another split is when agricultural land is subdivided to create lots for housing. Typically you can get four to six home sites per acre. Developers often double and triple their money in this fashion. However, as with other types of splits, there are pitfalls. Frequently you must drag utilities to each lot, which can be expensive. And the state may restrict the number of subdivided lots without special permission. For example, in California if you subdivide into four or more lots, you must file a map with the Division of Real Estate. One might think filing a map would be easy. But it's not. It provides for all sorts of things, from how you'll get utilities to the layout of the property. In some cases an environmental impact report is required. All of which is to say, if your goal is to split bare land, just be aware of the hoops you must jump through to be successful. Soliciting the aid of someone who has previously been successful at doing it and who can guide you is an excellent idea.

Can I change the use?

The most savvy of investors frequently make big bucks in land speculation by converting property from one use to another. For example, I have seen tremendous profits made when undeveloped land was bought and then resold later as prime industrial or residential lots. Initially, the land was worth a few thousand dollars an acre to the farmers who owned it, but, as developed land, it became many times more valuable. However, getting a change of land use usually requires approval of a county or city planning commission. It may go against the area's Master Plan. Or there may be legislation in place that prohibits the conversion of agricultural land within certain corridors. Finally, any opposition from neighbors, particularly if it is large and organized, will almost certainly doom the effort. If this is something that appeals to you and you have a likely lot as a prospect, contact a good local attorney who's familiar with the process and who can guide your steps.

What about rural/recreational lots?

Some of the most accessible opportunities in bare land exist in rural and recreational areas. These may consist of large lots (sometimes 40 acres or more) or developed parcels of only 10,000 square feet within a "country club" setting. If there's any sort of recreational amenity nearby, the lots could be golden. Today, a great many people are seeking second homes. They are looking for properties away from the crowded cities. Many desire vacant land on which to build their dream homes. The lots could simply be located in the woods, or perhaps by a mountain or stream. Because of their recreational value, their prices may be soaring. Many speculators, as a result, are purchasing such lots and simply sitting on them, waiting. When the price goes up sufficiently, they sell. Of course, the problems of acquiring such land (difficulties in financing) still exist. Nevertheless, it's often a better way to speculate in bare land. (The alternative is to buy land in agricultural areas, which can sometimes go decades without appreciating.)

Do I understand rural sewerage systems?

If you buy rural land, be aware that there are many traps to watch out for. One of the biggest involves sewerage. Unlike with city lots, there may be no municipal sewerage system. Rather, in rural areas, septic systems are commonly used. This involves a large tank, usually buried adjacent to the house, into which raw sewerage is dumped. From there, the liquids (called gray water) flow by gravity to a leach field where they are slowly absorbed into the ground. The cost of putting in a septic system today can easily be in the tens of thousands of dollars.

Am I aware of the potential problems with septic systems?

Problems can occur when the soil is not sufficiently friable to absorb the liquids. Or when the leach field is uphill from the house and a pump must be used. Or, far more difficult to solve, when there isn't enough useable land for the tank and the leach field itself. (Just because a lot is large doesn't automatically mean it's got enough room for a septic system. Typically the county sanitation officer will need to come out to render an opinion.) And today, most areas require the lot to be large enough for *two* leach fields, the secondary one in case the primary one fails. Finally, rural lots also often get their water supply from wells instead of a municipal water company. The well must be far enough away from the septic system not to be contaminated by it. Unless you're familiar with the utility problems, particularly that of sewerage, you might buy what appears to be a fine lot, only to learn later, to your dismay, that it's unbuildable because of a sewerage problem. Until you become savvy enough yourself, you should seek the advice of a good local real estate agent who specializes in rural bare land and who can clue you in to the traps.

Have I checked the property lines?

In urban settings, there are rarely questions about property lines. They are usually obvious and well defined by fences, zero lot lines (where the wall of one or more buildings is right on the property line), and other similar features. (Although, even in an urban setting, it's a good idea to get a land survey, which will tell you definitively where your lot ends and the next one begins.) In rural areas, a survey is absolutely essential. Fences are often placed on neighbor's properties. Driveways may meander on and off your subject property. Even houses can be placed erratically, sometimes with portions of them on neighbors' land. A survey will physically mark all boundaries of the property so that you can quickly see where the lot begins and ends. Further, a survey is often a first requirement by any lender (other than the seller) before getting rural financing. If there's a problem, try to get the seller to straighten it out before you purchase. Straightening it out yourself later on can be very difficult.

Will building costs be higher in rural areas?

The reason most people want rural/recreational bare lots is to build on them. Everyone seems to have his or her own dream house in mind, and this is an opportunity to create it. However, what few people realize is that building costs in such areas are often far higher than in urban areas. Extremes of hot or cold may require extra insulation and more costly construction. Putting in a road to the building site can be very expensive. (I recently had to put in a 300-foot driveway on a rural lot I purchased, and it cost almost as much as the lot itself!) Even excavation of a building site may be more costly if the land itself is hilly, is on a hardpan, or has boulders. Finally, reselling the lot (if you're speculating) may be made more difficult when potential buyers realize how costly it is to build on it.

18

Do You Understand the Investor's Tax Angles?

QUESTIONS TO ASK YOURSELF

Do I understand the nature of tax advice?

What follows is not tax advice. It is simply an overview of some of the federal tax rules affecting real estate investment property. It covers some tax breaks that may be available. Do not rely on this material. For tax advice you need to consult with a tax professional, such as an accountant or tax attorney.

Do I understand profit and loss from a tax perspective?

All of us want to make a profit. However, when we do make a profit, there's generally a tax to pay on it. Of course, with investment property you may be able to defer that tax through a "tax-free" exchange. Or you may be able to convert your property to a personal residence and get up to a $500,000 exclusion on capital gain for married couples filing jointly. If you have an investment property loss, you may be able to offset it against other investment property gains, or take it slowly against your personal income. Interestingly, if you show a loss on a personal home, you cannot deduct the loss.

When do I owe taxes?

You owe taxes when you realize a gain, basically when you sell. No matter how high the value of your property goes, you don't pay capital gains tax on the profit so long as you continue to own the property. You would, of course, owe income taxes if you showed excess income over expenses on an annual basis, and you would also owe property taxes.

Can I avoid taxes by trading my investment property?

You may be able to trade or exchange your investment property for another and defer the capital gain from the old property to the new. This is technically called a Section 1031(a)(3) tax-deferred exchange. Many investors use this as a means of multiplying their profits. They hop-scotch from property to property, increasing the value of their real estate holdings unencumbered by paying taxes on the gain for each transaction along the way.

Is a Section 1031(a)(3) tax-deferred exchange complicated?

Not exactly, but it is tricky. You would be wise to have a professional handle it for you until you know the ins and outs. The rules for a tax-free exchange were greatly simplified over a decade ago by several tax cases, the most famous of which is called the "Starker rule." Under Starker, you sell your investment property as you would otherwise. However, you have 45 days before or after the sale to designate a new property into which you will invest your money. And you have 120 days to close the deal on that new property. (You can designate an arm's-length entity—one that you cannot touch—such as a title insurance company escrow account to hold your money from the sale until it's ready to go into the new property.) Of course, there are other conditions of the exchange that must be met. One is that you may not take any cash out ("boot") as part of the sale. (If you want cash out, you must usually refinance the old property before the exchange, or the new property after it.) Another condition is that only "like kind" properties can be exchanged. This means that the property must be held for business or investment. It does not mean that you can only exchange, for example, an apartment building for another apartment building. Any real estate held for investment (house, apartment building, lot) can probably be exchanged for another.

What is the tax exclusion I've heard so much about?

After living in a property for a period of time (you must reside in the property for two out of the previous five years), you may then be able to sell the home and reap the benefits of the principal residence capital gains exclusion. It is up to $500,000 per married couple filing jointly, or up to $250,000 for individuals. It has some other conditions, however. For us the most important is that the property must be your principal residence. *It cannot be investment property*. The residence rule is strict. Thus, for an investor, this exclusion has limited value. Also, you can only do one of these exclusions every two years.

Can I convert an investment property to a residence and then take the exclusion?

Possibly. It has been done by investors. What you would need to do is to move into the rental property and reside in it for at least two out of the previous five years (assuming you hadn't previously done a tax-deferred exchange on it). Then, after the time period was up, you could sell it as a personal residence and take the exclusion.

What is the problem with a conversion and a tax-deferred exchange?

One of the problems many investors face is that they simply have no desire to reside in their rental property. So, they do a 1031 tax-deferred exchange (described above), and obtain a property they would like to live in. Then they reside in that property until the time limits have been reached and sell it as a personal residence, claiming the big exclusion. The problem here is that the government recently changed the rules. Now, if you previously did a 1031 tax-deferred exchange on the property, *you must reside in it for the full five years* before you get the exclusion. Apparently, so many investors were taking advantage of a combination 1031 exchange and exclusion that the government saw this as a tax loophole and moved to close it. While many investors are more than willing to reside in a home for two years in order to get the exclusion, far fewer are willing to do so for five years.

How do I calculate my capital gain when I sell?

You will likely owe taxes on your capital gain, therefore it behooves you to know how it's calculated. Basically, your capital gain on the property is the difference between the adjusted tax basis and the sales price.

Calculating Capital Gain

Sales price (adjusted for costs of sale such as commission)	$400,000
Minus Adjusted tax basis (described below)	250,000
Equals Capital gain (on which tax is due)	$150,000

Thus, to go through our example, your basis (discussed next) is $250,000. When you sell, after taking off the costs of sale (in this case $400,000), you subtract the basis from the adjusted sales price and that's your capital gain. The capital gains tax rate as of this writing is 15 percent for most taxpayers.

Can I depreciate my investment property?

You can depreciate investment real estate (the building, not the land). Here you consider a certain percentage of its "cost" (usually the purchase price plus transaction costs less the value of the land) each year as a reduction in the value of the property. Almost all business assets can be depreciated. Cars, for example, may be depreciated over a lifespan of 5 years. In a straight-line method, you might take 20 percent a year of the cost of the car each year over 5 years as a loss of value. Residential real estate usually must be depreciated over 27.5 years. Again, using a straight-line method (equal parts taken each year), you would take 1/27.5 of the cost each year as a loss. Remember: Only the building can be depreciated—not the land. Of course, the value of property usually goes up, not down. So how can you take a loss on an asset that's increasing in value? A helpful way to understand this is to think of it as a "paper loss." Most assets deteriorate over time. Even a house will eventually fall away to dust. So instead of simply waiting until the end of its useful lifespan (arbitrarily decided by the government), you take a portion of the loss in value each year.

Do I write off depreciation?

Yes, it's an expense like other rental property expenses, such as mortgage interest, taxes, insurance, water and utilities, and so on. But be sure to save all your receipts. In contrast to tax accounting for the home you live in for which the only deductions are typically property taxes and mortgage interest, almost everything is deductible for a rental property you own. You may be able to deduct a phone, auto, even business cards and other expenses you incur in managing the property. Check with your accountant.

Do I write depreciation off against my other income?

No, you can't do that. Rather, you write depreciation off as one of the expenses *against your rental income*. Since it's often a big number, it can frequently turn a property with a positive cash flow into one with a negative paper loss. Just remember that the loss from depreciation is not an out-of-pocket expense. It's simply an accounting loss—it shows up only on paper.

If my rental property shows a loss, can I deduct that loss from my personal income?

At one time depreciation was used by the wealthy to reduce their sizeable incomes. They would take the loss from their property primarily attributable to depreciation (it occurred only on paper) and deduct it from their ordinary income. That reduced their ordinary income, which, of course, reduced the amount of taxes they would owe on that income. That tax shelter was eliminated for the wealthy by the Tax Reform Act of 1986. Now deducting a loss is only available if your income is less than $150,000. The maximum deduction is $25,000 and you lose 50 cents for every dollar of that for income you make over $100,000, up to $150,000. However, in order to qualify you need to take an active part in the management of the property. See a good accountant on this one.

Why must I participate in management?

The Tax Reform Act of 1986 changed the rules with regard to real estate taxation. We now have three categories of income:

1. *Active Income.* The tax law now discriminates among the types of income that we receive. Income from wages or as compensation for services is called *active income*. It includes commissions, consulting fees, salary, or anything similar. It's important for those involved in real estate to note that profits and losses from businesses in which you "materially participate" (not included are limited partnerships) are included. However, *activities from real estate are specifically excluded.*

2. *Passive Income.* In general, *passive income* means the profit or loss that we receive from a business activity in which we do not materially participate. This includes not only limited partnerships, but also income from any real estate that is rented out. It's important to note that *real estate is specifically defined as "passive."*

3. *Portfolio Income.* Income from dividends, interest, royalties, and anything similar is considered *portfolio income*. We need not worry much about this here except to note that it does not include real estate income.

Under the old law, income was income and loss was loss. You could thus deduct most losses on real estate from your other income. Under the current law, your personal income is considered "active" while your real estate loss is considered "passive." Since you can't deduct a passive loss from an active income, you can't, in general, write off any real estate losses. The exception is for the small investor (income under $150,000 as described above), who materially participates in the property's management. If you own the property and are the only person directly involved in handling the rental—you advertise it, rent it, handle maintenance and clean-up, collect the rent, and so on—then, generally speaking, you materially participate.

What if I hire a property management firm?

This is a gray area. Generally, if you don't personally determine the rental terms, approve new tenants, sign for repairs, approve capital improvements, and the like, then you may not qualify. Many property management firms will offer to do these things for you. However, if you do them yourself, you're probably still okay. Remember, you will probably need to determine rental terms, approve new tenants, sign for repairs, approve capital improvements, and the like. If you are going to use a management firm, be sure that you have your attorney check over the agreement you sign with the firm to see that it does not characterize you as not materially participating and thus prevent you from deducting any loss.

What is the tax basis of my property?

Generally speaking, the basis of your property is what you paid for it plus some transaction costs. That basis is adjusted upward or downward while you own the property. It is adjusted upward by such things as putting on an addition. It is adjusted downward by things that reduce its value, most importantly here, depreciation.

How does depreciation reduce the tax basis of my property?

Once the tax basis is established for the property, it is used to determine the basis for the owner's gain or loss over time. If the owner sells the property, as we've seen, the selling price is compared to the tax basis to determine whether the owner had a capital gain or loss. Remember, the tax basis is lowered by the depreciation you take.

Change in Tax Basis due to Depreciation

Original basis (cost)	$300,000
Room added on	+50,000
Adjusted basis	$350,000
Depreciation (–$10,000 annually for 10 years)	–$100,000
New adjusted basis	$250,000

Notice that the basis was raised when an addition was made. But, over the years it was lowered as depreciation was taken. Keep in mind that the higher the basis, the less capital gain you will have. The lower the basis, the more capital gain. Therefore, although deducting a depreciation expense may seem an advantage in the immediate term, doing so will lower the tax basis in the long term when the property is sold and increase the amount subject to the capital gains tax, which will result in higher taxes.

How important is record keeping to me?

It's very important that you keep every receipt and note every expense and piece of income in a ledger. At some time you may have to prove to the IRS that the expenses you have reported on your investment property were real. For example, three years earlier you had a water heater go out and you spent $500 getting it replaced. "Prove it," says the IRS. So, you reach into your bag of receipts and pull out an invoice from the local plumber listing time and materials, including a new water heater for $500. That's very hard to dispute. Also, keep all records of any improvements you make to the property. Remember, improvements raise the tax basis, which will later reduce the amount of capital gains taxes you will need to pay. (The higher the tax basis, the lower the capital gain, and consequently, the lower the capital gains taxes.) If you make a capital improvement, such as add on a new room or patio, keep those receipts. At the end of the year, your accountant will be able to use them to adjust your tax basis upward. But also keep in mind that just because you spend money improving your rental, don't assume that you've made a capital improvement for tax purposes. Replacing a water heater, for example, is not a capital improvement; it's a repair. It will add to your operating expenses in the year it was done, but it will not add to your basis.

What if I refinance?

Refinancing your property without a sale should have no immediate tax consequences. You don't report new mortgages to the IRS. If you take cash out as part of a refi, you will, however, have less equity to rely upon later when you do sell and must pay capital gains taxes.

___

Should I become a "dealer in real estate"?

If you buy and sell many properties, particularly within a single year, the IRS may qualify you as a "dealer in real estate." What that means is that your profits are then all considered to be personal income, not capital gains, and the tax will be at ordinary rates. As a result, it probably will be significantly higher. Most savvy investors go out of their way to avoid being characterized as a dealer. Simply buying and selling a property once a year or once every other year probably won't qualify you as a dealer. Check with your tax professional.

___

Where should I go to get more information?

First and foremost, check with a tax professional such as an accountant or tax attorney. For more general information, check into my books, *How to Get Started in Real Estate Investing* (McGraw-Hill, 2002) and *How to Invest in Real Estate with Little or No Money Down* (McGraw-Hill, 2004).

19
Investor's Q&A Checklist

QUESTIONS TO ASK YOURSELF

Do I understand the principle of leverage?

Leverage is what makes real estate so profitable for investors. Consider the contrast with stocks. When you buy stocks you generally pay cash for the full amount. If you buy on margin, you will probably be able to borrow half the amount of the stock. When someone else puts up half the money, one of two things happens. You either can now purchase twice as much stock with the same amount of cash, or you only need to come up with half as much cash for the same amount of stock. Either way, you're leveraging your purchase. With real estate, lenders are willing to come up with 90, 95, sometimes even 100 percent of the purchase. That's far more leverage than any other investment I know. And it pays off when you sell. For example, if you buy a stock with 50 percent margin and the stock doubles in price, you've quadrupled your investment. If you buy real estate with a 90 percent loan and the price of the property doubles, you made 10 times your investment. If you don't believe it, an example should make it clear.

Leveraged Real Estate

Down	$ 10,000
Mortgage	90,000
Purchased rental	$100,000

Sold rental	$200,000
Less mortgage	−90,000
Less investment	−10,000
Profit	$100,000
Leverage	$10,000/$100,000 = 10 times

The leverage allows you to make the huge percentage of profit. And remember, the leverage can be even higher with higher LTVs (loan-to-values). Note: We've purposely overlooked transaction costs in our example.

Can I distinguish an "alligator" from a "cash cow"?

A *cash cow* is a property that produces positive cash flow—money into your pocket—each month. An *alligator* is a property with a high negative cash flow. Negative cash flow means you must take money out of your own pocket each month to cover expenses. (It's called an alligator because it "bites" you each month.) This usually occurs when the price of the property is out of whack with the rental income. This happens when prices appreciate far more rapidly than do rental rates, as has occurred in many markets in recent years. Here's an example. (Note: PITI stands for principal, interest, taxes, and insurance.)

Cash Cow versus Alligator

Cash Cow

Original market price	$200,000
Annual PITI expenses	−14,000
Annual rental income	+15,000
Positive cash flow	$1,000

Alligator

New market price	$400,000
Annual PITI expenses	−26,500
Annual rental income	+18,000
Negative cash flow	$8,500

Note that this is the same property. However, its value has doubled and for a new buyer, so have the mortgage costs. Rental rates have also gone up a little, but not enough to cover the new costs. At a price of $200,000, this property is a cash cow. At a price of $400,000, it is an alligator. Thus, to avoid buying an alligator you must not only check that the market price is correct based on comparables, but also that the rental rate is high enough to cover your expenses. This is not a problem if you're going to flip the property. It's a big problem if you intend to hold it long term.

Are condo conversions a good opportunity?

They can be. Here you convert an apartment building into condos. The opportunity comes from the conversion. For example, a single apartment's income may be $10,000 gross a year. Using a multiplier of 10, we learn that its sales value is $100,000. If you have 10 such apartments, you have a $1 million building. On the other hand, condos in the area with the same square footage as the apartment may be selling for $300,000 apiece. If you convert the rentals to condos and sell 10 of them for that price, suddenly your building is worth $3 million. You've tripled the building's value and increased your profits. It's not hard to see why condo conversions are gaining popularity. Keep in mind, however, that planning and building departments often impose strict regulations on conversions and, as a result, the conversion costs can be enormous. You might have to rebuild whole sections of the structure to comply with current codes. Moving existing tenants out may also be a problem in some areas, where you may be required to offer tenants first crack at the condos at a reduced rate. And because the apartment building is older, it may be more difficult to sell the condos than if they were brand new. Nevertheless, the potential profits are so high that many investors are wading in despite the risks.

Can I escape in a down market?

Wise investors know that things don't always come up roses. Thus, they have a plan for getting out of a property if things turn bad, which happened, for example, during the real estate recession of the mid 1990s when prices in many areas of the country dropped as much as 30 percent. When prices fall, if you are highly leveraged, you can quickly become upside down. That means that you owe more than the property is worth. Here are some typical escape plans that investors have used.

Escape Plans

Dump It.   When prices level off, before they begin to decline, the investor quickly sells the property, even at just break-even or a slight loss. The idea is to avoid waiting too long—sell before you get upside down.

Hold It.   If the property comes close to breaking even (not an alligator as explained above), the investor forgets about flipping, forgets about reselling, and hunkers down for the long haul. Over time, real estate has always rebounded and the property will undoubtedly go up in value, eventually.

Second It.   Sometimes, in order to facilitate a sale in a down market, the seller/investor can offer a second mortgage to allow a weak buyer to come in with virtually no down payment.

Wrap It.   It may be possible to wrap this second mortgage around an original first, so there is no need for a very weak buyer to qualify for any new mortgage. Most first mortgages, however, have "due on sale" clauses that prohibit wraps, so you must be careful.

Lease-Option It.   Here, you essentially rent the property to a tenant who has the option of later buying it (see below). It can be an effective way out. Be aware that lease options are restricted or prohibited in some states.

Contract It.   A contract for deed (also called a *land contract of sale*, see below) allows you to retain title while the buyer has time to gather up enough money to make the purchase. Be aware that land contracts are restricted or prohibited in some states.

Should I use lease options?

The lease option is a method of selling property, most commonly used in a down market. It involves leasing the property to a hopeful buyer along with an option to buy at a set date and usually at a set price. A portion of each month's rent is applied toward a down payment. At the termination of the lease, when, hopefully, the down payment has been reached, the buyer gets a mortgage, and the sale is completed. With a lease option you can have all the problems inherent in renting, including maintenance and the possibility of having to evict the tenant for nonpayment of rent. These risks, however, can be minimized by getting a hefty security deposit and by carefully screening the applicant, making sure that your tenant has a previously successful rental history. The advantage is that you can get a buyer who might otherwise not be able to purchase the property to buy it from you. The causes of most problems with lease-option arrangements are that the amount of the rent that goes toward the down payment is not sufficient, or the tenant/buyer cannot qualify for a mortgage to complete the purchase when the term of the lease expires. One solution is to get the person preapproved for the eventual financing before renting out the property. In that way, you have some assurance that the eventual buyer can qualify for financing. You will also learn just how big a down payment will be needed and you can adjust the rent accordingly. Problems with this approach are that interest rates fluctuate and people's credit standing changes. The buyer who qualifies today may not tomorrow. Note: Some states have restricted or even prohibited the lease option—check with a good attorney in your area.

What about using a land contract of sale?

A *land contract of sale* (also called a *contract for deed*) is an old form of transferring property used for years in bare land sales where the buyer couldn't come up with the full purchase price in cash. The seller gives the buyer a contract to buy that states if and when the buyer ultimately comes up with all the cash, title will be transferred—no cash, no title. During that time the buyer usually can work or occupy the property. Today, the land contract is still used by investors to purchase properties that they otherwise can't get into, and to sell properties that they otherwise can't get rid of. Some of the reasons for using it include the following.

Reasons for Using a Land Contract

- To give the buyer time to come up with the cash while protecting the seller from giving title to a property not paid for.

- To avoid lawsuits. A buyer who is being threatened by law suits will sometimes acquire property using the land contract. Since the contract is not recorded, the buyer's name is not on the property, and in a lawsuit that property is less likely to become involved.

- To attempt circumvention of the alienation (due on sale) clause in modern mortgages. Since the contract is not recorded, the lender may not learn about the transfer and may not demand the mortgage be paid. This is a dangerous tact.

On the negative side, the contract of sale is often an insecure position for a buyer. If the seller of a property decides that he or she wants to be dishonest, he or she can sell it again, even after it's first been sold to you. Since recording of title is the means by which ownership is determined, and since a contract of sale is not usually recorded, this is possible. Today, in many states a contract of sale can be recorded if at least one party that signs it has that signature notarized. Further, some states now restrict or prohibit land contracts.

Should I form an LLC when I invest?

Some real estate gurus advise setting up a *limited liability corporation* (LLC) as a means of protecting yourself from liability when investing in real estate. On the other hand, most real estate investors I know just go for it, using their own names. One thing to consider is financing. Most lenders I know are hesitant to make the same kinds of loans to an LLC as to an individual. They want that individual to be on the line to make those payments. They don't want someone who feels he or she can just walk away. I'm sure an LLC can shield you from some liability issues. However, when there's fraud, as has been the case with some overenthusiastic flippers who got appraisers to overappraise values and were not

completely candid with sellers and rebuyers, it is probably of limited value.

Do I fully know my sources of investment cash?

When you need cash for a down payment and closing
costs, the easiest thing to do is to write a check. However,
when you don't have the money in the bank to back it up,
that's not an option. Here are some alternatives for raising investment cash that you may not have considered.
Keep in mind, however, that whatever you borrow must,
presumably, eventually be paid back. And investing in
real estate is not risk free. Never use any funds you need
elsewhere, such as for living expenses or retirement.
Never gamble with money you can't afford to lose.

Raising Investment Cash

Line of Credit. Most banks today have all sorts of plans
that allow you to establish a credit line. It can be as
simple as an overdraft on your credit card to a revolv-
ing credit line on you house. Many banks offer non-
collateralized (no security except your name) lines to
their better customers. Consider establishing and
using one of these.

Savings. You've got that account saved for a rainy day.
If you can live without it, consider spending it on
real estate.

Stocks and Bonds. With the way these markets have
been performing, liquidating them and putting the
money into property might be a wise decision.

Rarities. Many people have coin collections, paintings,
sculptures, and other forms of rarities. If you can
part with them, and if they haven't been showing
strong price appreciation, consider selling and moving the money to real estate. eBay offers excellent
opportunities for disposal of such assets.

Bullion. Many people keep gold, silver, platinum, and
other precious metals in a vault or safety deposit box
as a safeguard against a rainy day. Maybe it's raining
now and you should consider using the assets to
purchase property?

Refi.   A good many investors got their starts by refinancing their existing homes, taking money out, and buying more property. If you have multiple properties,
sometimes you can get a blanket loan to cover all of
them and cash out.

Move.   If you're serious about buying investment real
estate, consider selling your present home and moving to an apartment for a while. You could then use
the money to reinvest in commercial real estate.

Borrow.   Rates are currently low. Try your bank or credit
union. They may be willing to give a low-interest
loan. Just be sure you get the money months before
you invest in real estate so that when you go to a
property lender, you can honestly say you aren't borrowing the down payment.

Credit Cards.   Yes, cash advances are very expensive.
You could be paying 20 percent interest or more. But,
if you only need the money for a few months, it
might be worthwhile. If you're going to borrow on
high-interest credit cards, always be sure you have a
realistic plan for replacing the borrowed money with
a low-interest real estate mortgage.

Friends.   Many younger people today have close friends
who would do almost anything for them. Consider
borrowing from them. Just be sure you have a pay-
back plan.

Relatives.   Relatives tend to be less forgiving than
friends. If you borrow, be sure you make it clear
what it's for and the risks that are involved. It's a
good idea to have it all written down on paper, just
in case Uncle Bill has a memory lapse.

Gifts.   Relatives and friends may be willing simply to
give you an outright gift to help you get started in
real estate. Parents do this all the time to help their
children get into a home.

Sell.   We all have assets we can live without, though it
may be painful. It could be a boat, a piano, a motor-
cycle—whatever. Decide what you want more, to get
started on your fortune in real estate or to have the
pleasure of the moment.

Do I have the right temperament to be a real estate investor?

A good real estate investor needs a variety of personal assets. These include the following.

Personal Assets Needed

Attention to Detail.   It's hard to imagine any line of endeavor where lack of attention to detail is an asset. You'll find that you need to keep track of market values, rental payments, and all sorts of numbers. A good ledger (or PDA) will help. But it's still up to you to remember the details.

People Person.   It's hard to imagine any line of work where personal interactions aren't important. You should be able not only to sell your property, but also to sell yourself to lenders, sellers, and buyers.

Integrity.   This is a must in any profession. Keep your word, pay your debts, and don't harm others. Keep to these guidelines and it's hard to see how you won't succeed.

Index

About the Author

Robert Irwin is one of America's foremost experts in every area of real estate. He is the author of McGraw-Hill's Tips and Traps series, as well as *The Home Buyer's Checklist, How to Get Started in Real Estate Investing*, and *How to Buy a Home When You Can't Afford It.*